# GROWING THROUGH JOY

## ULLA SEBASTIAN

First published in 1999

ISBN 1-899171-67-3

British Library Cataloguing-in-Publication Data.
A catalogue record for this book is available from the British Library.

Layout by Pam Bochel
Cover design by Phoenix Graphics

Printed and bound by WSOY, Finland

Published by

**Findhorn Press**

The Park, Findhorn,                 P.O. Box 13939
Forres IV36 3TY                     Tallahassee
Scotland, UK                        Florida 32317-3939, USA
Tel 01309 690582                    Tel 850 893 2920
Fax 01309 690036                    Fax 850 893 3442
e-mail: info@findhornpress.com
http://www.findhornpress.com

## DEDICATION

*I dedicate this book to the Findhorn Foundation*
*the garden*
*that provided me with the fertile ground*
*for fast and rapid growth*
*the hall of human mirrors*
*in whose reflections I discovered who I am*
*the global community*
*that gave me the opportunity*
*to share my love and wisdom*
*and to serve the core*

# Contents

# Acknowledgments

So many people have crossed and shared my life's path and taught me to grow with joy that it is hard to single anybody out. People have been my major teachers: my clients and workshop participants who shared parts of their life with me and helped me to understand and appreciate life's journey from suffering to joy; my trainees who grew with me over many years and became colleagues and friends; the many guests from all over the world who kept me informed in my B&B in Findhorn and made me aware about the awakening that was happening in so many places on the planet; the friends who have been with me, supporting me in the dark times of transition and encouraging me to keep moving forward through the wheel of life.

Among the many I would like to express my special thanks to my dear friends Carmella Sutherland and Jill Brierley, whose continuous encouragement helped me to move from one stage of growth to the next, with whom I could share the cosmic giggle and laugh whole-heartedly at our own shortcomings, whose intuition and deep understanding of the universal laws has been a constant inspiration and invaluable help. I am deeply grateful for their friendship, love and support that is accompanying me wherever I go.

I would like to extend my gratitude and appreciation to Dianne Falasca with whom I have worked for many years within the educational stream of the Findhorn Foundation. She held me through all my doubts and tears around my own life's purpose, while we were assisting others to realize and live theirs.

Many men have passed through my life, teaching me to smile through the pains of misunderstanding and hurt. They have strengthened my will and ability to take charge of my life, to step into my power and to live life to its fullest. To all of them, my thanks for all they taught me. I would like to especially extend my gratitude to Crawford Kemp who has been a friend and teacher, a playmate and partner, and a spiritual companion on the path. He has taught me to see and experience life from a different angle of the world, extending and enriching my capacity to embrace the different approaches to life.

A special thanks also to Sigrid Fontana who has been following my path for many years, encouraging me to step out into the public sphere and to share my experience and knowledge. With patience and perseverance, she has been reading and correcting the many versions of this manuscript. Her suggestions have been an invaluable help in bringing this book into its present form.

Over the last 25 years there are many friends who have been with me at different times in the cycle of my life. We are in the habit of spending intense times together, and then moving on along our separate paths until we meet again for another intense patch of the road. Among them I would like to express my gratitude to Marlies Luethi and Dieter Erbe, Christa Fritze, Barbara Mettler von Meibom, Brigitte Gross, and Susanne Winkler. whose presence and friendship provides me with a continuous vessel of support and nourishment.

I have learned from many people whose dedication to humanity and this planet has advanced the human consciousness and who have been an enriching inspiration to my concepts and thoughts. I would like to especially thank Chloe Wordsworth whose ceaseless dedication to her work and her life's purpose is a continuous inspiration for my own work.

The tool that she put together, the Holographic Repatterning, has enriched my own life and the life of many people I have worked with.

The Findhorn Community in the northeast of Scotland has been a tough school of rapid learning that took me to the edge of choosing suffering or joy. There aren't many places that are prepared to take us to the depth of our being, especially if the path is rough and uncomfortable.

Within this context, I would like to express my limitless and unbounded gratitude to the 'other school' that is held and run in the other dimensions and, to me, is the guiding force of the Findhorn community. The 'other school' of the ascended masters has convinced me over time of the unconditional love that is available to us if we let go of our own pre-conceived ideas about the course of our lives. I am deeply grateful that this 'other school' never gave up on me, despite my complaints and stubbornness, and that it brought me back to the path whenever I was ready to quit.

I am very pleased that this book is published by Findhorn Press. I am grateful to Karin and Thierry Bogliolo for their support and encouragement and the ease and joy of our cooperation together. They have been colleagues at different stages of the road as we all moved through different roles within the Findhorn community. I am delighted to continue the cooperation beyond the confines of the physical community in Scotland.

My special thanks also to Tony Mitton, my English editor who took on the task of bringing my non-native English into a smooth and readable style. His comments and suggestions have inspired me to re-write parts of the German text, realizing how my understanding had grown during the year's space between the German and the English version.

And a special thanks to Pilar Basté, my Spanish publisher, whose courageous dedication to the task of bringing the wisdom of the ages to the people has opened the door for many. That knowledge and wisdom has also nurtured and sustained my own life.

Most of all, I would like to acknowledge my parents who have lived through two world wars, and for the courage and the strength with which they lived their lives within this dark century. They taught me to never give up, to continue the journey and to trust that there is a light that will rush in to help us in our darkest hours. The deep wisdom and quiet simplicity of my father and the fast, sharp and curious mind of my mother challenged me to find a synthesis between these two ways of life, and sharpened my awareness of the many ways in which people express themselves. They were invaluable motivators in exploring the depth of the human psyche and the human mind. I would like to extend my gratitude to my brother Helmuth and his wife Marita for their support and presence when we had to join forces to support my parents in the predicament of aging. It fills my heart with delight that we joined together in mutual support and love to do what was needed to help them cope with the aging process and the changes that this brought to their lives.

*Our deepest fear is not that we are inadequate. Our deepest fear is that we are powerful beyond measure. It is our light, not our darkness that most frightens us. We ask ourselves, Who am I to be brilliant, gorgeous, talented, fabulous. Actually, who are you not to be? You are a child of God. Your playing small doesn't serve the world. There's nothing enlightened about shrinking so that other people won't feel insecure around you. We are all meant to shine, as children do. We are born to make manifest the glory of God that is within us. It's not just in some of us; it's in everyone. And as we let our own light shine, we unconsciously give other people permission to do the same. As we're liberated from our own fear, our presence automatically liberates others.*

*Nelson Mandela*

# Introduction

They are peculiar roads, those which lead us forward through our life and into new and unknown territory. They often come from different directions, cross our path at places where we least expect them and open views onto unknown terrain. Often, we recognize their significance only when we look back and see how they have woven themselves into the pattern of our life.

The skillful traveler recognizes the signs that beckon us when we lose our orientation and get lost, or reach important junctions and do not know where to go. Such signs can be events, encounters or words which appear like answers to our questions. They can be thoughts and ideas that emerge out of the blue, or memories that shine a sudden light on our current position.

My own life is full of such coincidences, junctions and encounters. Also, I have searched in very focused manner for answers to recurring questions. I have described a part of this journey in my book *Erfahrungen bei Sai Baba in Indien*.[1] Today, twelve years after I wrote that book, some of those events appear in a new light. And I have found answers to the questions which I could not answer then.

Twelve years ago, words like God or spirituality were still disreputable in my circle. It took a risk, as many of my friends made me feel, to write about somebody like Sai Baba or even to write an autobiographical report. To give up a professorship and to join a spiritual community was not only shocking to my parents; many of my friends thought me lost in the swamp of spiritual dependencies.

Today the landscape has changed. To search for the deeper meaning of life is not an alien idea any more. Books about spirituality and personal development overflow the market. In the face of ecological disasters, economic inequalities in the world and the epidemic spread of chronic diseases like cancer and Aids, many people are asking themselves how they can bend this threatening fate towards the preservation and improvement of life.

Change begins with each one of us. It begins with you. If you change, the world changes. Why?

---

[1] Ulla Sebastian. *Erfahrungen bei Sai Baba in Indien (Experiences with Sai Baba in India)* (German text). München: Goldmann 1992

We are all tied together. As in a gigantic web, each impulse starts a vibration that continues through the whole spinning network. Each thought, intent and act is an impulse. What you think and do has an effect. It is up to you what kind of impulses you send.

You have a choice between impulses that constrict and destroy life and thought forms and behaviors that invigorate and enhance life. You may not be conscious of this choice. Many people act out of their unconscious programs.

The first step therefore is to become aware that each one of us *has an effect*. Then you can choose *what* kind of result you want to achieve and *how* to set about it.

Consciousness includes all those aspects. We need to understand the impact that we as humans have on life. We need to recognize the laws that govern the consequences of our choice and we need the knowledge of how to apply those laws in daily life. This book deals with all those aspects.

Carl Gustav Jung, the renowned Swiss psychoanalyst, made us aware of the different ways people perceive this world. He distinguished four types among us. We can use either our sensory perception or intuition to access information, and either conceptual thinking or feeling to make sense of it. According to our individual preferences, we either think or feel the world, and we either focus on details or the bigger picture.

In life we need all four faculties. We bring to our lives a natural disposition towards one or two of them, and we explore and familiarize ourselves with the other ones through our life's course.

The type of knowledge or techniques that attract us depend on the preferences we bring with us. I am personally drawn to the intuitive-mental realm. I am a visionary. I love philosophy. I like to understand the essence of life, the essence of this world and the essence of this universe.

I have spent the last ten years in a spiritual community in the Northeast of Scotland, at Findhorn. Most people there are my opposite. They perceive the world through the intuitive-feeling mode. They approach life through personal contact. They are interested in people and their story, not in concepts and universal laws.

I became aware of this fact when one day a representative of the London Institute for Psychosynthesis approached me. He asked whether I would be willing to teach the course about 'Theories of Human Nature' for the training group in Findhorn. I hesitated and requested time to think about it.

The subject of the course was familiar, but how on earth should I teach theory to intuitive-feeling people? They 'hate' categories and generalizations.

I had an intuitive flash. How about looking at the life-stories of the 'big' thinkers of our time and explore their theories and concepts as answers to their life-questions? In that way, theory would become alive and would not just be a sequence of dry, abstract systems. This approach was new to me. Fascinated, I read the life-stories of the famous scholars of human consciousness, such luminaries as Sigmund Freud, Carl Gustav Jung and Wilhelm Reich, and I explored the questions that motivated them to find the answers which have become world renowned. The more they became alive as human beings, the more profoundly could my students connect with the knowledge that these persons have contributed to the development of human consciousness.

This experience confirmed an observation I have made during my therapeutic work over the last thirty years. Some people need to understand the concept before they are willing to commit to a deeper work. Others need to experience how a method 'feels'. Some intuitively grasp the principles while others need a lot of detailed explanations.

The difference between these approaches to life confronted me with the question, how could I best present you with the knowledge that has become available to me during the last decades? This knowledge covers modern scientific reasoning and old esoteric knowledge. And it includes practical, hands-on guidelines of how to apply this knowledge to your daily life. As we often learn by example, I also want to bring in case material and my own life's experience to blend all those different aspects together in an easy-to-read mixture.

So, I invite you to accompany me on my expedition into the secrets of life and share my questions and answers. You are welcome to use them as inspirations and practical guidelines for your own journey.

A word of warning. You do not need to understand the theoretical considerations in order to profit from the exercises and instructions of this book. The principles of the work are simple and you can use most instructions without previous knowledge. Use what makes sense to you, forget what does not appeal to you, and grow with what inspires you. Each person has his own individual path.

Have a good journey through the book.

# From Suffering To Joy

## Searching For The Key

I remember as vividly and clearly as if it were yesterday that hour in my bedroom loft in my newly built house. Backbreaking months were just over. I had undertaken the maddening attempt to build an ecological house without possessing the necessary financial resources. I had trusted that the laws of manifestation, on which the Findhorn community[2] is based, would also operate in my case. The law of manifestation is a universal law. It instructs us how to bring a thought, an idea or a concept into material reality. You will hear more about it later in this book.

It did not take long to find out that the practical application had its pitfalls. Despite all my efforts, all possible sources of finance had been exhausted towards the end of the building project. I could no longer afford to hire my builders. I had to take on part of the interior work myself. In no time I acquired new skills, like painting wooden frames and floors, tiling, and sealing walls. Time ran short. The summer was close, and I had hoped that many guests would stay in my new B&B. Just in time for the pre-determined deadline, on my 45th birthday, I opened up the guest house.

Now I was sitting in my loft, looking back at the months that I had just left behind. Those months had been filled with struggles and doubts whether I would manage to generate the money for the materials and salaries in time. On top of all the work in the house, I had run seminars, developed models for a new integration of the Findhorn community and negotiated between its different parts. I was used to doing several things at once, but this combination had exceeded my capacities by far.

I had repeated the pattern of a lifetime, knowing that I was repeating it. I had overstretched myself to the point of total exhaustion. This time I had done it so thoroughly that I had reached bottom. Gain and loss cancelled each other out.

---

2 The Findhorn Community is an international educational center and spiritual community in the Northeast of Scotland. It was founded by Eileen and Peter Caddy and Dorothy McLean in 1962.

If we reach the bottom of a pattern, we come to a choice point. We can continue our behavior until we start to destroy ourselves, or we shift and choose a road that takes us out of the pattern. The decision at this point is up to each one of us.

"It is enough," I said to myself. "Enough of the struggle and the effort. There must be another way to grow than through agony and tears. From now on I will grow through joy."

Said and done? Yes..., and...

I started to explore the kinds of things that would nourish the germ of joy and let it thrive and blossom, and the things that would threaten it.

I found out that it was enough to remind myself that it had been my choice to build the house, to establish a B&B and to give consulting sessions. This reminder removed the sense of heaviness that sometimes weighs on me when I have to hold too many people in my awareness. I had chosen these circumstances. Therefore I could change them. This thought enabled me to go forward with new courage and joy.

I noticed that my energy level rose when I gratefully acknowledged all that I had created and all that was given me, instead of focusing on those things that were missing. I affirmed that it was my pleasure to share my house, my experiences and my knowledge with other people. The more joyfully I did that, the more people felt drawn to me.

I discovered the healing power of responsibility, gratitude and service in my daily life, and the nourishment they provided for the expansion of the heart and the cultivation of love and joy.

However, at the same time I found myself sinking into old habits which endangered the germinating seed of joy. The old habits had power and often proved to be stronger than the wisdom and knowledge which told me how to cherish and cultivate the seed of joy.

I understood that it was important to let go of the old and to make peace with my life's story. I started to peel off the layers and clear the way to deeper and deeper ground. The process seemed endless, like a spiral staircase that winds beside the same old stones.

I discovered that I had the choice to move either up or down the spiral staircase, down into the suffering or up into the joy. The suffering had its attractions. I learned that it was dangerous to underestimate its power. It was too well established in the same cultural patterns and milieu in which I felt at home.

I was not the only one to experience this phenomenon. My clients seemed just as incapable as I of following the path of joy, despite their best intentions and all their knowledge.

I wondered what it is that holds people in the chain of suffering, even against their better knowledge and their best intentions. What I had so far learned on my therapeutic path gave me no answers. The reason had to lie deeper.

I found two books which broke new ground for me: Vernon Woolf's *Holodynamics* and Michael Talbot's *Holographic Universe.* In my sessions with clients I began to understand the role that inner images, or holograms, play within the stream of human consciousness. They steer the course of life from the Unconscious, despite all our good intentions. I started on an adventure trip through the jungle within in order to track them down and understand and use them for the positive power of life.[3]

I noticed that my clients' lives took a turn for the better when we succeeded in understanding what gift their present problem brought to their situation. The issue became an ally instead of an adversary. The conflicts, which usually originate from the friction between our inner traits, dissolved, and harmony and inner peace emanated instead.

The aim of the process is to draw the energy out of the old dynamics patterned on suffering and to use this life force to nourish the new sprout of joy. The more the new plant thrives, the easier it becomes to penetrate the old forms and to transform their power into healthier modes of being. In the course of the work some fundamental steps emerged, which I will discuss in the sections about the Basic Pulsation of Life and Holographic Analysis.

I was astonished by the power that came out of the transformation and maturation of those inner images. At first, I didn't know how to explain this phenomenon, although I saw its effect daily in my sessions with clients. Then I came across Chloe Wordsworth's work about Holographic Repatterning. Instead of inner images, she uses pre-formulated statements as guidelines, and instead of intuition, a muscle checking procedure. Despite these differences in procedure and technique, the results were amazingly similar. I was fascinated.

---

[3] I owe many insights and a solid training to my inner 'team' of guides that has accompanied and taught me during the last 30 years of my work.

The more I worked with both these approaches, the more I began to grasp the world of resonance. I understood that each process, indeed all of life, is a vibration through which the universe expresses itself. Each thought, each feeling and each behavior has a frequency. The same frequencies attract each other. "In the beginning was the Word," proclaims the Bible, and the word is a vibration.

The emotions of anger, fear, guilt, doubt and shame have a lower frequency; joy, unconditional love or compassion for all sentient beings have a higher frequency. If we want to change our resonance with the life-depleting emotions and beliefs, it should be enough just to focus on joy, love and compassion and to cultivate them, as the great teachers of mankind have told us through the centuries.

Energy moves to the place where our attention is focused. This is a natural law. If we direct it towards the higher frequency of love, we move ourselves out of the lower frequencies of fear, guilt and doubt.

If it is so simple, why do we not do it? What hinders us from applying these simple laws to our situation and leading a healthy, fulfilled and happy life?

The answer is simple... and complex.

We are part of the stream of the evolution of consciousness, a great stream that has been flowing for millions of years. Each person is part of it. Each contributes in their own way to this current, but we are all at different places within it.

Some people listen to their insights about the universal laws and apply them. Many of us must first prepare the ground. We are attached to the cultural stereotypes and our attitudes are determined by fears and insecurities. We need stepping stones to help us trust our own power and fortify our courage enough to release familiar territory and explore the unknown. The last section on transformation contains instructions on those small steps which empower us to take charge of our lives.

One of my heroes is Beppo, the street-cleaner in Michael Ende's novel, 'Momo'.[4] He sweeps the infinite street. However, he does not look towards its end. He sweeps stroke by stroke. One day he looks back and the street is swept.

---

[4] Michael Ende: *Momo*. Stuttgart: Thienemann 1973

If I look at my life, I can recognize myself in Beppo. And there are many people whom I encounter on my life's path who have the same experience. Through many little steps we discover that we influence our life towards the Good or the Bad.

Like Alfred D'Souza, you can consider obstacles as problems:

> *For a long time it had seemed to me that life was about to begin – real life. But there was always some obstacle in the way, something to be got through first, some unfinished business, time still to be served, a debt still to be paid ... then life would begin. At last it dawned on me that these obstacles were my life.*

Or you can see obstacles as chances to grow. It depends on your inner attitude whether you sweep the street with suffering or with joy.

Life is composed of individual steps. To live is to grow. Growth is like a pendulum movement which can swing into higher or deeper planes. You decide if the way leads upwards into the vibration of joy and love, or downwards into fear and narrow-mindedness.

How do you decide upon the course to take? Your decision is determined by the nourishment you give yourself. Nourishment is the information which you incorporate, the people with whom you surround yourself and the thoughts that you think all day. If you predominantly take in information that has to do with suffering, or if suffering plays a major role in your thoughts and relationships, you risk becoming mentally crippled. If your 'food' is invigorating and heartening, you grow in contentment towards the life that you wish for yourself.

Growth is inevitable. If you refuse to take the steps voluntarily, life presents you with circumstances that force you to move forwards or change direction. That is the experience of my own life and the lives of those people that have shared a part of their path with me.

If growth is inevitable, then why not grow through joy? This is a quiet joy which is independent of circumstance. It is not that explosive, exuberant feeling which you see on advertisements for washing lotion and tooth paste. It is more of an inner knowing, emanating from a state of trust that a source greater than ourselves is taking care of our life. In physical life it is not possible to avoid grief, for instance at the loss of a parent. Yet beneath either sorrow or those sparks of happiness and bliss that fill our cup to overflowing with wonder and awe at life's bounty, joy remains. It is a quiet assurance and knowledge of the inner divinity which fills the whole being with a state of steady tranquillity and peace.

Joy is the quality of the heart which we build as we grow in our capacity to take responsibility for life; to be grateful for what is given and to let go of what is no longer needed; and to expand our capacity to love and serve others.

## Addicted To Suffering

In the course of my therapeutic work, I became aware of a phenomenon that I call 'addiction to suffering.' Thomas is an example.

A year before he came to see me, his life had taken a sudden and surprising turn. He had moved into another house. This move was the beginning of a long chain of events in which his life had collapsed. He had worked himself more and more into a state of shame, guilt and the feeling that he was a failure. He had gone to different therapists for help and had found open and compassionate hearts, but nothing had improved in his world within. On the contrary, it had become worse.

As we examined his problems, it became clear that they presented no existential threat. On the contrary, the sale of his house had improved his financial situation, though not his marriage or his personal well-being.

While I listened to him, I saw a small, inquisitive boy who did not dare show himself under the crushing burden of self blame. I showed him how his posture and breathing pattern helped to maintain this condition, and how he could gain a realistic estimate of his situation by changing his breathing pattern and grounding himself. This gave us the base from which to explore the gift that was hidden beneath his self-accusations. On a symbolic level, the self blame took the shape of a gigantic flint with sharp, cutting edges. By holding onto them he could gain a sense of safety and stability. This stone had grown during the year and seemed to overpower and suffocate the flame that was his true symbol.

In the course of our work he recognized how his wailing and complaining had pulled him down deeper and deeper into a spiral with power so strong that all resistance seemed vain. He had become addicted to suffering.

This story reminded me of times in the Findhorn community when 'woundology'[5] was the common ground of communication. In endless meetings, participants shared the wounds of their childhood, and yet talking about them did not resolve them. On the contrary, one's misery proved to be an excellent way of gaining some sympathy and love without having to change anything in one's situation. Wounds served to create a sense of identity and communality until the destructive side became evident to everybody.

This experience in the collective repeated what I had learned years before in my therapeutic process. At the beginning of my training in Bioenergetic Analysis, I had had the idea that I could overcome my suffering if I went deeper and deeper into it and finally came out on the other side. Joy seemed like a trophy to be achieved as a reward for successful suffering. But the deeper I dug into the morass, the worse it became. My therapists supported me in this process and helped me find out more and more details. It took me many years before I realized that I had landed in a dead end. The reward at the end of the winding path through suffering was not delight or satisfaction but an adjustment to it.

It is important to distinguish between pain and suffering. Pain signals an injury or an imbalance in our system. Suffering is a fixation on the pain, an attitude of ignorance or an attempt to find an identity. Suffering can also serve as a defense mechanism and prevent one from being confronted with the real pain. Unfortunately it also prevents healing from taking place.

One of the most difficult of life's demands is the ability to 'stand in the wound', especially in the 'wound of love' which is the ultimate wound. Many people feel helpless and powerless in the face of misery, especially if they are confronted with the whole spectrum of human violence and destruction. It is hard to endure our sense of helplessness and powerlessness through to the point where new life can burst through. Instead, we tend to avoid our feelings by engaging in activity or by entering into the 'collusion of suffering'.

Collusion in my understanding means the unconscious co-operation between people. Take for example a personal conversation between two friends. A large part of the conversation revolves around problems. On the surface, it seems that both are searching for a solution to unresolved issues

---

[5] I owe this term to talks with Carolyne Myss

or unmet needs. As we look closer, we see that sharing their suffering serves to attract attention and sympathy. Neither of the two sides is seriously interested in making any decisive change in their lives. I call this structure 'collusion'.

Another instance of collusion in esoteric circles is the common custom of quoting the opinions of friends or the reading of an astrologer or the Tarot to support one's opinion. These serve to legitimize one's situation by affirming that one's plight is not one's own fault or responsibility. 'The stars already tell..., and others say as well ...'

This is not to say that Tarot or astrology are damaging in themselves. I use them myself to gain insights into the bigger picture. However, if they are used to clothe one's story with the garments of victimization and to retreat from personal responsibility, they miss their true function.

As a model for my work, I take the custom of an Indian tribe which was once told to me. In this tribe, no one is allowed to tell the same story more than twice without taking concrete steps to change their situation. If the person comes back a third time without having taken any such steps, the doors close. The other members consider such behavior an exploitation of their time and goodwill.

Imagine that custom in the subculture of woundology. Relationships would become a desert. Or something would actually change!

The expansion of the therapeutic realm over the last three decades has contributed a good deal to the development of woundology. In an effort to understand and dissolve a person's blocks, the therapist has actually encouraged the client to go deeper into their suffering. Then, instead of setting the energy free to pursue new positive goals in life, the suffering has turned into a life strategy. The wounds were not cured, but have served to set up a new identity for the person as victim or sufferer.

The collusion of suffering gives both therapist and client the illusion of working on the issues while preventing healing from taking place. Who would exchange a wound which grants so much identity, recognition and social reward within the subculture of woundology, for an indefinable and hardly conceivable healing which requires self-responsibility and self-discipline?

Many of the sixties generation who set out to change the world now find themselves at a dead end. The big jump entailed in changing our culture from its pre-dominantly intellectual and technological bias to an orientation of the heart is happening at a slower rate and in different ways than they expected. The question remains, how do we get out of the dead end and move on?

# From Lack To Abundance

In our culture, suffering is closely connected to the concept of lack. Coping with conditions of lack has marked the history of mankind. Lack, or the opinion that our resources are limited, has determined our political, social and psychological systems. The sentence, "There is not enough" is closely connected with the sentence, "I do not have enough" and "I am not enough," or in the more popular version, "I am not good enough." With this basic attitude, a person strives not to lose.

How different a life would be if it took its stand under the motto, "I can win?" Let us do an exercise:

**Exercise**

➤ Close your eyes for a moment and allow yourself to feel the different impact of two contrary points of view.

▷ *Become aware which energies get mobilised when you attune to the sentence: "I can win. I just need to decide to do it."*

*And then notice how this sentence affects your body: "I must take care that I do not lose."*

➤ Can you feel how in the first case your energies expand, and in the second case they contract? Can you sense how the thought of losing oppresses your heart?

Winning in this context does not mean that another person is going to lose. Win-lose-games are part of the toolbox of lack. Can you imagine situations where everybody wins? Where profit means that your intentions and actions serve others as much as yourself?

To grasp the difference, you need to change your viewpoint from lack to abundance. Joy is a principle of abundance and expansion. And abundance is the growth principle of the universe.

If you look at nature, you'll notice that it is overflowing with abundance. Each spring, life springs forth in an extravagant diversity of forms. Each seed produces a hundred new ones. Each species generates new nuances and variants. Cells divide and multiply. Old forms pass and new ones emerge. Life sustains life and expands it.

Look into the universe and you find millions of suns and galaxies. Space has a limitless potential. Space has no boundaries. Space is expansive.

The universe follows the law of evolution. It develops from simple to more complex forms that themselves represent a higher order of the simple forms. The laboratory of nature bubbles over with diversity and profusion.

Nowadays we can clearly recognize this trend in the computer-industry and communication technology. The development of microprocessors has enabled a world-wide spread of personal computers. They are the "hardware system" that allows a global communication-network to unfold. The acceleration rate of this process is greater than most people can imagine. Just look at the speed at which your computer becomes obsolete and you get a sense of the speed of the change.

The success of computer technology is partly due to the fact that the engineers successfully reproduce the processes of nature. Nature applies the same principles over and over again, no matter whether it deals with macro- or microcosms. As above, so below; as within, so without; that is the law. Each part includes the whole.

It is in our mind and with our brain that we set limits to our thinking. Our thinking is historically programmed towards lack, towards having or not-having. In the past, having or not-having decided who won the battle of survival. In the model of the Either-Or, we are either victims or perpetrators. If we land on the side of the victims, we qualify for the dynamics of suffering.

Only in the last two decades are we becoming aware that we can win, grow and learn together. With this understanding we move from competition to co-operation. We understand that we need to work towards creating abundance for all instead of distributing the lack.

## The Guilty Universe

### HE DIED FOR OUR SINS

Have you ever wondered, when you go into a church, why Jesus Christ is usually shown suffering on the cross?

I have wondered about it all my life. It made no sense to me that his suffering, crucifixion and death seemed so much more important than the more encouraging evidence of his resurrection. If I look back on the scriptures which were read in church, I rarely heard anything about the resurrection and even less did I understand. What stayed with me was the notion that I am guilty, and that Jesus had died for my sins.

As a child, I couldn't make any sense out of this statement. Why should somebody have died 2000 years ago because of my little missteps? Nevertheless, the guilt-feelings were all pervading, deep and incomprehensible. Many years would pass before I could even begin to understand what the guilt-feelings, suffering and resurrection were all about.

The God of my childhood was a mighty God. Nothing could escape him. He had his eyes everywhere. He was a God external to me, and yet at the same time he was sitting inside me like a giant spider which holds everything in its grip. He was an inescapable God, sometimes merciless if I had offended the social law governing what 'One does', sometimes a comforting God if life seemed too difficult.

He was a God of sin, guilt, disgrace and shame. As such, he was a God of disempowerment and control. Guilt keeps people in servitude, especially if that guilt is in no way proportionate to any concrete act and therefore cannot be amended. The church based a whole system of power and control on the notion of sin and its associated guilt. We fool ourselves if we believe that our technological society has grown out of it. The roots lie deep and reach far into our collective psyche.

Being human means being fallible. In my understanding, to be human means that one has the right and privilege to make mistakes and learn from them. Without this permission one cannot grow. The claim that we should be already perfect makes us inhuman and lies at the root of many depressions.

There is a difference between people who realize their goals in life and grow through joy, and those who are attached to suffering. The difference stems from the way they perceive the problems with which their daily life confronts them. The first group sees them as exciting challenges from which they can learn and grow. The others use them as yet another proof of their own incompetence. Not the facts of life, but how we see them and what we make out of them, determine our reality.

The culture in which we grow up influences the individual's perspective. If we believe that at the end of life, heaven or hell will await us depending on how often we have offended against the religious laws, fear will determine our life. This has the more impact, the more the collective mind carries the traits of an omnipotent and punitive God.

Fear means constriction, and constriction does not allow us to learn from mistakes and unfold our potential. Fear and guilt are intimate relatives. They catch us in a life spiral which downdrafts deeper and deeper into hopelessness.

### THE SINS OF THE FATHERS SHALL BE VISITED UPON THEIR CHILDREN

If you are tormented by guilt-feelings that do not seem to relate to your life or actions, it may well be that those guilty feelings are not yours. Guilt-feelings are energies which get passed on from adults to their children. Up to puberty we are exposed to the energy field of our parents or other adults, and we are vulnerable to what they pass on to us. In my sessions, clients often find out that they carry the guilt-feelings of their parents, their grand-parents and their ancestors. Whole generational chains come into being supported by the Christian philosophy of the sinful and guilty man who can only be saved from outside, through God's mercy.

If we become conscious of the fact that the guilt which we carry is not ours, it is much easier to release it. Sometimes the guilt is such a large element of our own identity or inner reality that it cannot just be dissolved without further ado. We must first fill the gap left by its removal with positive energy. In my therapeutic sessions I use symbols or colors for the purpose.

**Exercise**

▶ How would you feel if you could simply shuffle off this load which you carry around? Who would you give it to? To the source from which everything originates? To God, Christ or the universal mind? Can you imagine that? How would it feel?

Perhaps you say it would be a liberation. But that is only one aspect. At the same time it is the loss of an old and familiar friend. All parts of your personality, no matter how burdensome, also serve you. They are the mechanisms which helped you overcome difficult situations in your life, mostly in childhood. They will only be willing to release themselves if you appreciate and value them for all that they have given you. If you do this, the energy that is tied up in those patterns can return to you. You are then free to use this energy to create whatever you want in your life.

In the section about Holographic Analysis, I will give examples of these steps.

## HEAVEN AND HELL

If you look at Jesus' life from the perspective of the resurrection, the cross takes on a different meaning from that of suffering.[6] From this viewpoint, the cross symbolizes the possibility of overcoming death. Jesus overcomes it through the knowledge that the father and he are one. If we realize that we as humans are one with the universal mind, death becomes an illusion. Death is not an end or the destruction of life, but the transition to another dimension.

---

[6] I owe this perspective to Eugene E. Whitworth's excellent book: *Nine Faces of Christ*. Marina del Rey: DeVorss 1980

The cross and the suffering are intimately connected. Our language expresses this connection in sentences such as, "Life is a cross" or "Everyone has their cross to bear." Just as the crucifixion represents a step towards overcoming death, so suffering is a step towards recognizing that we can just as well grow through joy. It symbolizes that life does not have to be an effort and a burden, but can be fulfillment and love.

For most people who are programmed to experience lack, this step is difficult. The one-sided view of the cross as a symbol of suffering has rooted the fear of death into our flesh. This fear is closely connected to the fear of a Judgment Day which will bring bliss or condemnation. In the Christian view, the Court of Judgment is an external authority which will ultimately punish us for our sins.

From reports about near-death experiences,[7] we know that people on the brink of dying are confronted with a life review which is very similar to the court scenes of the world religions. However, unlike the predictions of religion, the people in transition are not condemned by light beings but by their own judgments stemming from their own feelings of guilt and remorse. Whether and how people experience Judgment Day depends therefore on the beliefs that they already held in their lifetime.

The people who have had near-death-experiences report that they perceive the presence of the light beings only as love and understanding. The light beings advise them of the importance of love and self-knowledge, and how vital it is to put one's work into the service of other people.

In the Christian view also, the service of others is a central determinant for one's own bliss. However, this service is connected with moral obligations and renouncing the satisfaction of one's own needs. The Christian guiding principle, "Love Your Neighbor as Yourself," forgets far too readily the second part, "As Yourself." Consequently, serving easily turns into helping. Helping arises from motives other than love or the knowledge that we as mankind have to evolve. We will learn more about this in the section about service.

As you can see, our partial perspective which sees the cross as a symbol of suffering has far-reaching consequences which pervade all aspects of life. The abbreviation of Christ's teachings to sin, guilt and suffering causes people to submit responsibility for their life to external authorities. And

---

[7] Compare Michael Talbot. *The Holographic Universe*. New York: HarperCollins 1991, chapter 8

together with the responsibility, they submit their power and their independent thinking. Losing those, they easily become victims of the power interests of others and subject to manipulation by public opinion.

The Christian view of the world is deeply rooted in our collective psyche and so is deeply rooted in our internal dynamics too. Even those who are not members of a Christian church and who believe in progress and technology are confronted by this same theme.

The Christian perspective is not the only one that is conceivable. It is not even the philosophy and life style which is most appropriate to human dignity. We turn therefore to the wisdom of Eastern traditions and the knowledge of modern science.

# The Conscious Universe

## THE UNIVERSAL MIND

Buddhism has impregnated the thought processes of the people in the Eastern part of the world, and differs from Christianity in its outline of the relationship of humanity to the universe.[8]

According to Buddhism, our fate is directed by no external God, but by the Consciousness of whom we are all part. God in this view does not exist outside of us, but is our essence, our very nature. As part of the universal mind, we partake in creation. In consensus and harmony with this consciousness, we create our reality. Consequently, our responsibility for our life is different from that in the Christian-Catholic philosophy.

As part of the universal mind, we do not need an external organization to take account of our being and doing. We are committed to ourselves, to our own inner essence. The Protestant outlook with its concept of conscience comes closer to this understanding than the Catholic ethic. Buddhism and Protestantism differ however in their idea of Good and Bad.

Just as in the Catholic Church, Protestant ethics are branded with the idea of sin, of right and wrong. When our deeds do not conform with its ethical

---

[8] I owe the inspiration for this section to Sogyal Rinpoche: *The Tibetan Book of Living and Dying.* London: Rider 1992

principles, remorse rather than the penance imposed by the priest will punish us. The penalising authority is different, the belief in sin and punishment is the same.

I still remember the sentence from my childhood, "The Dear God sees everything". His gaze was inevitable and merciless even in regard to little white lies and slips. Faced with remorse, I had to judge soundly which was the lesser evil, to be punished by my parents or by the 'beloved' God in the form of merciless and pursuing remorse.

In the Buddhist understanding, the universal mind is not a moral authority. The universal consciousness does not judge or sentence. Judgment separates its pristine unity. Judgment divides and every division produces polarity. We humans tend to turn polarities into contradictions. Each polarity thus carries the germ of a conflict.

A contradiction expresses the viewpoint of the 'Either-Or.' In this view, if your partner is right, it automatically implies that you are wrong. And since you do not want to be wrong, conflict starts. On a higher plane of consciousness the contradictions dissolve. On these higher levels of consciousness, different viewpoints can both be legitimate. The 'Either-Or' turns into an 'As-well-As.'

On the highest level of consciousness, the plane of the universal mind, there is no separation. The universal mind is ONE, a primordial ground, an undivided foundation, an absolute truth. Humans, just like all other creatures, participate in this absolute truth through their individual viewpoints or their relative truths.

Your relative truth is no better and no worse than mine. If we stop to compare, we stop fighting each other. If we stop fighting each other, we start to see and appreciate what each relative truth contributes to the understanding of natural laws. In this way we unite instead of separating the ONE.

A core principle of life is karma, the law of cause and effect. Each thought, word and deed sets things in motion. Each thought, word and deed has an effect. When your thoughts are filled with anger and hate, the effect is to bring events into your life which confirm that anger is justified. If your thoughts are filled with anxiety, you attract what you fear.

What is true for the negative is also true for the positive. If you fill your heart with joy and love and cultivate those qualities, you attract joy and love. You decide what you cultivate. You cultivate what you think. It is up to you which qualities or events you want to bring about in your life.

Cause and effect in the Buddhist view are not the same as in the Newtonian Scientific World view. Traditional science attempts to comprehend the phenomenal world and to define causes and effects within this material level of existence.

One example is the medical model. Within its parameters, we consider microbes such as bacteria, viruses or fungi as the cause of infections. A broader psychosomatic understanding would also include emotional well-being and thought processes in the cause category. From the spiritual perspective however, there is one Consciousness who is the life behind all the phenomena of the physical world. The universal mind produces it all, physical, emotional and mental well-being. In this understanding, the world without, the phenomenal world, is a mirror of the world within.

## THE CONSCIOUS AND UNCONSCIOUS MIND

The individual mind has two ways in which to operate, through the conscious and unconscious processes. Both shape the inner world. Both are activities of the individual mind.

Our conscious mind acts like an information gatherer. It collects information from the exterior world through the five senses of sight, hearing, taste, smell and touch. If its activity is not controlled by conscious choice, it checks this information according to our old programs and selects those which confirm our beliefs and convictions.

Turning to the unconscious mind, on the physical level it regulates the vital processes which preserve and sustain life. Among these are the sexual functions which ensure the survival of the species, the maintenance functions such as respiration and blood circulation which keep the body vibrant and healthy, and the functions which protect the body from harm and disease.

On the mental level, the unconscious mind is the storehouse of memory. It contains all the experiences that have been passed on to us over the generations or that we have stored in response to events in our life. These reactions are often connected with intense feelings. They hold the memories in place and determine our day to day behavior. The unconscious is the seat of habits. It is the robot which relieves us of the task of thinking up our routines afresh every day. Our life is conditioned in much more vital and central ways than we would like to admit.

On the spiritual level, we find in the unconscious the source of our creative power, which is the power to control and direct life in harmony with the universal mind. This intuitive channel expresses itself in intuitive flashes or bursts of spontaneous wisdom that suddenly open new connections to our view. This divine spark has inspired pioneering scientific breakthroughs like Einstein's theory of relativity and Jonas Salk's discovery of the vaccine against polio.

We can intentionally tap into this source and use it to create our life and future. To do so, we need to become aware of the capacities of our mind and apply them according to universal principles.

Through the five senses, our mind provides us with information from the outside world, and through introspection and intuition, with data from the inner world. The objective is to select, focus and direct this information consciously.

To do so, our mind needs to be able to distinguish what information is important and what is irrelevant. Our priorities determine what is important to us. Most people make their decisions without much consideration, since they are not aware of their power and capacity for conscious choice. They are driven by programs rooted deep in the flesh which interpret information in such a way that they confirm and strengthen old thought forms and behaviors.

## THE LAW OF ATTRACTION

The cosmos operates according to the law of attraction. This states that 'Like Attracts Like.' The mind has the ability to attract. This is because the mind is energy, and energy expresses itself in vibrating wave patterns of different frequencies. All energies will gravitate to energies of similar vibratory rates.

Matter consists of vibrating wave patterns of energy. All thoughts, attitudes, feelings and behaviors vibrate at certain frequencies of energy. Each attracts ideas, people, circumstances, events and things that resonate in harmony with its wavelength.

Take anger as an example. When you were already fuming, has anyone ever taken the parking lot from just in front of your nose? Or on another occasion perhaps, you were insulted for no good reason and later got involved in an accident? Or do you remember situations in which you were already feeling victimized, and then you actually met people who took advantage of you or trampled on your feelings?

Because these events seem to happen through external circumstances, we do not notice that we have produced them. To put it more precisely, our attitudes and survival responses stored in the unconscious attract the events and situations which resonate with them, and in this way control our life.

## THE POWER OF THOUGHT

Our mind can use the law of attraction in our favor. The ability to do this lies in the power of creation. Its tool is the thought process.

Edgar Cayce said thoughts were tangible forms, entities of a subtle form of matter which have the power to determine our fate. Buddha said, "We are what we think. Everything which we are emerges from our thoughts. With our thoughts we create the world." The bible teaches us: "Faith can move mountains". And Paramahamsa Yogananda recommended his disciples to create the future by using visualization. Through practising concentration and willpower, the right visualization enables us to materialise thoughts not only as dreams or visions in the mental realm, but also as experiences in the material realm.[9]

Just as we can attract negative forces into our lives through our unconscious beliefs and thoughts controlled by our previous programming, so we can attract positive outcomes into our life by using conscious control and choice of direction. The principle is simple: you create in yourself the vibratory frequency which brings what you wish for into your life. As within, so without. If you want health, visualise your body as completely healthy. If you want more love, give more love. If you want prosperity, expand your abundance within.

By focusing on the positive side of life, you express your willingness to take the necessary steps to reach your goal. If you aspire to complete health, this may mean that you should inform yourself about nutrition, fitness programs or relaxation techniques, and then do what is needed. If you wish to receive more love, your first step may be to give yourself more love. By balancing the feeling of lack, you create a better base for love in yourself. That allows more love to enter you, which you can then share with others.

---

[9] Quotes from Michael Talbot: *The Holographic Universe*. New York: HarperCollins 1991, chapter 7

It is the privilege of the human race to have free will in harmony and in accordance with the laws of evolution, be it as a species, a society or a person. You can choose to dig in your heels against the flow of life, or to attune your personal will to the universal mind and there work with ease and grace. You can choose how to create your life, who will be your companions, and which seeds will bear fruit.

It is said that it is up to each one of us how we interpret our present reality, what we attract and what we achieve in our lives. If the kind of life we create is up to us, why do so many of us create a life of material or emotional misery?

## KARMA AND RESPONSIBILITY

In the Buddhist view, our life is one of a sequence of many from which our soul gathers different kinds of experiences. The effects which we set in motion do not end with death, but according to the law of cause and effect they continue in the next life. Consequently, we are not an empty page when we enter this life, but we bring with us imprints which impact its course.

Earlier in my life, I had often wondered why the same kind of incidents continued to happen to me, despite all my precautions, insights and changes. My personal story was a chain of wrecked relationships with men.[10]

In the course of time, as I pondered on the repetitive nature of these events, I became aware that life confronts us with particular lessons which appear in different guises. They are key events which point us the way to our inner core. Since these events are often painful and entail a lot of suffering, I found it first impossible and then difficult to perceive them as positive. From my own work with many clients, I know how resistant people are to the idea that their material, emotional or mental misery may be a reflection of their world within and a signpost to the true self. It seems much simpler to blame it on others.

However blaming others does not save us from the suffering. If we take on responsibility for our agony and misery, if we therefore accept ourselves as the creator of this condition, then we may accept that we can just as well create a good and fulfilled life. We can choose to do this with grace and ease or effort and torment.

---

[10] I have extensively described this process in my book: *Erfahrungen bei Sai Baba in Indien*. München: Goldmann 1992

Many people in our culture believe that something is only worthwhile if it takes effort and work. It is as if they need sufficient agony stamps before they can grant themselves the good things of life.

We need to become aware that this thinking is part of our Christian inheritance and is not the law of the Universal Mind. In the conscious universe, the responsibility is laid in our own hands.

In this context responsibility means freedom, the freedom of choice. As is pointed out in the section about choices, we are confronted with a choice on each level of our development. If we do not choose to meet the choice consciously, we choose restriction, disturbance or suffering. This may last for years until we reach the point where we make the decision in favor of our personal well-being and the well-being of all. And... it can happen right now, in this moment.

What's important is that you have a free will. You choose. Here and Now.

## THE JOURNEY 'BACKWARDS'

The art is to go into the stillness, relax, let go and arrive where we already are. The process therefore is not so much a new learning but an 'unlearning' in the sense of releasing our programming. It is a journey backwards, as Bhim S. Goel calls this process in his book *Psychoanalysis and Meditation*.[11] In the stillness on this journey backwards, we look piece by piece at the programs which determine our life. By liberating them from the restraints of the unconscious and by moving them into the light of consciousness, they dissolve. If the soul recognizes their message and integrates them, the old structures have fulfilled their task. The journey backwards guides us from that which we think we are, back to the original spiritual source of whom we really are.

To track those patterns, we need to practice looking at them. Psychoanalysis is the methodology which has explored that path most systematically and profoundly in the west. The Eastern tradition has equipped us with insight meditation (Vipassana) which trains us to become still and to direct our attention to the perception of our thoughts, feelings and body sensations. We have to submerge into the deeper layers of our existence because most of our motives are unconscious. Our conscious thought processes are only the tip of the iceberg.

---

[11] Compare Bhim S. Goel: *Psychoanalysis and Meditation*. New Delhi: Paragon Enterprises 1986

Between our conscious will and our unconscious motives there is often a contradiction. The body-mind system executes the instructions of both the conscious and the unconscious mind. It possesses no critical ability to discern between the messages. If the instructions contradict each other, confusion and chaos result. Since the world without is a reflection of the world within, we then manifest inner chaos in our environment, our relationships and our work.

## THE CONTROL OVER THE THOUGHT PROCESS

An essential step is to harmonize our different parts and to unite them behind a common goal. For that, we must become conscious of the thought process so that we attain control over our thinking, and with it over our individual consciousness.

The word control needs to be explained. If you think of the people who in your opinion are controlling, you will probably have noticed that they are often stiff and not very flexible. Their control serves as a defense against their fears or feelings of insufficiency. These people control out of their fear of the unknown and unexpected. They try to ignore or shut out all that is uncanny from their life.

I do not suggest that we control our thinking after this manner. It is a basic feature of the creative mind that its ways are often unforeseen and lie beyond our present imagination. Control in this context means that as a first step, we take precise notice of what we are thinking in each moment and accept the diversity and multitude of the thoughts just as they are.

When you have gained experience in following the ceaseless stream of your thoughts as a passive witness, you can actively start to impact this stream and strengthen those thoughts which you would like to find as outcomes in your life. To the same degree that you cultivate positive thoughts and feelings, you replace the negative thoughts and feelings. The dark and the light cannot exist simultaneously. It is in the nature of things that the dark is consumed by the light.

If these thoughts are new to you, then accept for a moment that the world without is a mirror of the world within. If you look at your situation in life from this perspective, you can gain an insight into some of the imprints that you have brought into this life. These imprints are not only your individual ones, but are also influenced by the cultural and social conditions under which you grew up. All the people in my circle of friends who were influenced by the Christian culture have to deal in one way or another with guilt. Guilt-feelings are deeply anchored in our collective psyche.

Our personal experiences and responses to our life events are embedded in the collective unconscious. These experiences are a web of viewpoints, emotions and bodily structures which inescapably seem to run our life. We swim around in them like a fish in water, a creature which is so much part of its element that it cannot recognize its own nature.

In fact, many people live as if they are in an aquarium which they perceive to be the only possible reality. Only if the events of life hurl them out of it are they forced to look at this aquarium more precisely. Distance is necessary in order to look at life from the perspective of a witness, without judgment and without identification.

Control over our thinking is a long process composed of many small steps. The way from the aquarium to the ocean needs practice and experience, like everything in life. The prospect of suddenly having to survive in the big ocean would only fill us with fear and panic, and rightly so. The ordinary mind, so say the tantric mystics of Tibet, functions like a pond which is separate from the ocean.[12]

The important point to recognize is that we are part of a much bigger mind and that our thoughts are the material which determine our fate. We weave our future through our thinking today. To shape what we want, we need to give our thoughts attention, concentration and focus. We need to utilize consciously the forces with which we unconsciously bombard and confuse ourselves.

## The Holographic Universe

How can we gain control over painful and repetitive patterns? This question has engaged me for a long time. Through psychoanalysis and my training in Bioenergetic Analysis, I investigated the motives which entangled me over and over again in unhappy relationships with men. However, all the knowledge and all the insight gained did not translate into action. I could not find the button which would have switched off the old programs.

---

12 Compare Michael Talbot. *The Holographic Universe.* New York: HarperCollins 1991, chapter 7

During my years in the Findhorn community in the northeast of Scotland I began to research more systematically. I wanted to know where the mechanisms are stored that direct our life and how we change them in such a way that they loosen their power over our life. I had a clear inner image of the process: up to now I had only worked on the ripples which a stone makes when one throws it into the water. I had not yet advanced to the stone itself.

## THE POWER OF INNER IMAGES

At the beginning of the nineties I came across a book by Vernon Woolf called *Holodynamics*. Therein he applies the knowledge of quantum physics to the work on our inner traits. The book fascinated me, although I did not understand much of it. However, one idea stuck with me: the possibility of making immature patterns more mature. Woolf called these patterns holodynes. Holodynes are thought forms which are equipped with an independent existence within the store house of our memory. They have the power to set events in motion. They are the software for our behavior or feelings.

These holodynes are shapes which control the flow of our thoughts and feelings deep within our consciousness. If we change the shapes, we change the stream. For example, if we are conscious of the shapes which attach us to suffering, we can transform them into the higher vibratory frequency of joy. We transform the stream of suffering and fear into a stream of joy.

In my work with my clients I began to explore the world of symbols and metaphors. Symbols and metaphors are the language of the unconscious. They are images which tell an event or a story. Two renowned psychoanalysts of this century, Sigmund Freud and Carl Gustav Jung, have decoded these images within the setting of dreams and collective archetypes.

I discovered that if my clients asked their body symptoms or behavioral patterns to take a shape, their meaning and function for a particular event became evident. Furthermore, they lost their power over the client if we succeeded in preserving their positive function in a healthier form.

Let us take a bodily symptom such as a headache as an example. In such a case, I ask the client to ask the headache to take shape. The image that comes up may be a large black block or a closed room. Together with the client I explore what 'gift' this black block or room presents for him or her. The most frequent gift is protection from outer demands. In the positive sense, the block gives permission to withdraw into one's own room, or to refuse to do things which feel like an imposition.

I was surprised how effectively these inner images and metaphors expressed the experience, and how their transformation opened the way for new views and different actions in the outside world. I developed a spectrum of simple techniques to shape and transform these inner patterns and will present them in the last part of this book. I call the approach 'Holographic Analysis'.

After a few years of research and working with these metaphors, I came across a second book which pointed me in a direction similar to Vernon Woolf's book about Holodynamics. In his work, *The Holographic Universe*, Michael Talbot presents results from some of the more recent realms of science.

## THE REALITY AS HOLOGRAM

The concept of the Holographic Universe is based on the concept of the Hologram. A hologram is a three-dimensional picture that looks like an actual object. However, you can walk right through it. It has no physical limits.[13]

A hologram is produced by a pure light source, like a laser beam, which is split in two by a beam splitter. The first beam reflects off the object, in this case let us say an apple, onto a photographic plate. The second beam reflects off mirrors onto the same photographic plate. Both beams together create criss-crossing wave patterns. They are called interference patterns.

Imagine yourself throwing two stones into a pond of still water, making waves which ripple outwards and cross each other. They create a pattern of wave mountains and valleys. This corresponds to the interference pattern of the two laser beams.

When you let a third laser beam shine through the interference pattern on the photographic plate, a three-dimensional image of the object appears on the other side. This is the hologram.

---

[13] I owe the inspiration for the following section and diagram to Michael Talbot. *The Holographic Universe*. New York: HarperCollins 1991, Chapter 1

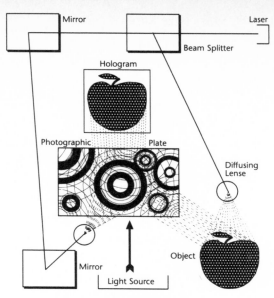

**Figure 1: The Hologram**

The interference pattern on the plate contains many sections of the photographed object or situation. According to the angle from which you let the third laser beam shine through the plate, you receive different images of the object or event.

If you apply this phenomenon to a human being, the third laser beam corresponds to your intention. Depending on your viewpoint, aspiration or desire, you create a different reality. If the viewpoint is impregnated by suffering, you create a different reality from that if you were to perceive the same situation from the angle of joy. The popular language expresses this phenomenon in the image of a half-filled glass. The pessimist describes it as half-empty, the optimist as half-full.

Another remarkable characteristic of the hologram is that each part contains the whole. If you break the picture into pieces and let a laser beam shine through just one part, the whole picture appears.

If we apply this phenomenon to our everyday life, it means that each sensory impression can call forth a whole picture or a whole memory. For instance, for many people the smell of coffee triggers a feeling of home and comfort, since the smell is connected with coffee and cake in a circle of cherished friends or family. A table outdoors in the sun in front of a restaurant calls forth images of beautiful vacations in the South. A remark can bring up old pain, or you may meet a person whose movements remind you of a dear friend.

According to the understanding of brain scholar Karl Pribram, memories are not stored in a specific place in the brain. The brain cells, called neurones, have tiny branches over which they pass along messages in the form of electric impulses. At the end of the branch they distribute themselves like waves which cross each other and form interference patterns and create a hologram. They can be activated through each of our senses and so enter our conscious mind.

The brain can produce illusions which resemble a hologram, for example, pain in limbs which have been amputated. We know from psychological research that a large part of what we perceive as reality does not exist at all in the outside world, but gets supplemented by our brain according to previous experience. This explains why witnesses who have observed the same accident or criminal event often give different stories and tend to be unreliable.

The American mathematician Benoît Mandelbrot calls the capacity of a hologram to create orders within orders within orders, a fractal dimension. He illustrates this by using a computer graphic that has been named after him, the Mandelbrot-set. He translates a simple mathematical formula into a computer produced graph that looks like a turtle. You can go into each aspect of this shape, from the large picture down to the minute detail, and the turtle appears over and over again.

Fractals are the method which nature uses to create abundance and profusion. This approach is contrary to our established way of thinking which is to solve a problem by doing more of the same, only harder. Fractals create more with less. It is like driving a car when you change gear at a certain speed. If you are driving at 40 miles per hour and you use the third instead of second gear, you achieve more with less energy.

When our system becomes overloaded with information or work, we tend to respond with more work and effort. We do more of the same, which, from a certain intensity on, leads to burn out or system breakdown. Nature manages this problem by spontaneously shifting to a higher level of complexity. It uses simple, repetitive structures and with these produces a higher or more complex form. Just think of the 'roses' of the cauliflower. They are composed of many enfolded hills and valleys. And all the 'roses' together form the cauliflower. The same principle applies to the human brain. The universe unfolds from the simple to more and more complex levels of existence.

## UNFOLDED AND ENFOLDED REALITIES

What we perceive as reality is not the only possible reality. Pointing to a different view, quantum physicist David Bohm describes the interplay between unfolded and enfolded orders. What we see and experience as 'real', which is the unfolded order, is basically an illusion. It is comparable to a holographic picture. Underneath, there is a deeper level of existence that extends itself beyond time and space.[14]

Between both levels of reality there is a continuous interplay, a constant, flowing exchange. The observer determines by his viewpoint, intent and interaction which facets of this continuous stream become visible or remain invisible. All the things in our reality that seem to be separate and singular are but brief manifestations within an indivisible wholeness, into which they sink back again when their time is fulfilled. David Bohm calls this continuum a holomovement, a constant stream which continually changes and shapes itself. Within this stream, units take on a unique shape and at the same time remain part of the river. Think for a moment about the swirls in a river. Each swirl has its particular features such as size, direction and rotational speed, and yet you cannot say where a swirl stops and the river begins.

Examples of the existence of a deeper level of being that lies beyond time and space are to be found in the psychic phenomena of clairvoyance or intuitive knowledge. Among these phenomena are precognition, retrocognition and telepathy. Precognition sees things in the future, retrocognition events from the past. Telepathy is the ability to communicate with other people or beings across the boundaries of space. A fourth area which we do not comprehend with our normal senses is psychokinesis, meaning the ability of certain people to move objects in a room merely by their presence.

Such events have been reported time and again, and many times rejected as not scientifically verifiable. Nevertheless, you may have had a personal experience which leads you to credit the possibility: perhaps one day you were thinking about somebody you had not heard from in a long while, and the next day you get a letter from them; or you think of a person, and the

---

[14] Michael Talbot. *The Holographic Universe.* New York: HarperCollins 1991, Chapter 2

next moment you meet them; or suddenly, in an inner vision, you see yourself in another place, and a couple of years later you find yourself in that precise spot; or, if you enjoy working with plants, you may have found how they flourish better if you speak to them, or please them with beautiful music.

Carl Gustav Jung has called the coincidence of unusual events 'Synchronicity.' The term expresses his belief that coincidences are not accidental. More than that, 'Synchronicity' is a statement that we are all part of an indivisible whole, and that our thoughts, attitudes, desires and intentions set in motion things in the material world and that they apprehend events beyond time and space.

## THE WEB

Used in respect of mankind, this word signifies that we are all part of the same indivisible material out of which the universe is made. Whatever we think, feel or do, it has an effect on others. And since we are part of the same continuum, our actions ultimately return to us. This is the deeper meaning of the sentence, that we reap what we sow.

These are scientific insights which are not new. Again and again, from their various perspectives, the great teachers of mankind have pointed us to this web, but up to now we have lacked the capacity to grasp or reiterate the universal laws in a scientific way. Fa Tsang, a Buddhist master, described the web as a multidimensional lattice of jewels which are all tied together and reflect each other in infinity.[15]

From this perspective, biblical commands change from the demands of an external authority to become conclusive guidance on how to unfold our life to our best advantage. Just take the sentence, "Do unto others as you would have done to you." If you know that ultimately all your thoughts and deeds will return to you, you will examine much more precisely what you wish for or do to others.

The knowledge that each of us is a unique jewel in this giant web has a still further consequence. It means that each individual is important. What each one of us thinks and does has an effect. Each of us makes a difference, be it good or bad. Thereby, we become deeply responsible for the life that we create, not only for ourselves but for the next generation and the preservation of the planet as a whole.

---

15 Michael Talbot. *The Holographic Universe*. New York: HarperCollins 1991, Chapter 2

## CREATING THE FUTURE

From this perspective, life is not an inevitable fate. If everything is contained in everything else, past, present and future are not a linear happening as the structure of our brain wants us to believe. They happen simultaneously. From this aspect, time is more appropriately compared to the skins of an onion than to a stretch of road which leads from A to B.

It follows from these considerations that we can cast a glance into the future and even influence this future. You may have heard about people who were warned in a dream not to take a particular airplane or undertake a certain mountain hike. And in fact, the airplane crashed or the people on the hike met with a fatal accident. Evidently many people have the ability to intuit the misfortune of such events beforehand. In his book about the Holographic Universe, Michael Talbot reports that nineteen people foresaw the sinking of the Titanic. Some took the presentiment seriously and survived, others ignored the message and drowned.

If it is possible to see and shape the future, how then does our free will relate to Destiny? To what extent is the future pre-determined and how far can we influence it?

According to the information that Michael Talbot gathered, both aspects play a role.[16] Each hologram is pre-determined and allows us to recognize what the future has in store for us. Tony Cordero pictures the future like a hurricane which gradually forms, gathers strength and becomes inevitable as it comes closer. If the event is still far enough in the future, we can decide to step out of this hologram and into another. This is what happens when, because of his presentiment, somebody does not take a certain airplane or calls off a particular project. The future is enfolded within the present reality. In other words, it is hidden within the deeper order. It is like a hologram which is substantial enough to be perceived by us and flexible enough to be changed.

In my own life I experienced this relationship with the future when, at the age of 33, I went to an Indian Yogi for the first time in my life. He looked into my right hand and pointed to a scattering network of delicate lines at the end of my life line. "You have a serious life crisis ahead of you," he said. "I will die from cancer in my forties", I answered to my own surprise. Until

---

[16] Michael Talbot. *The Holographic Universe.* New York: HarperCollins 1991, Chapter 7

then I had never thought of it. He nodded his head and remarked: "If you succeed in averting this fate, the life line in your hand will grow clearly and strongly through the network of these thin lines."

As the readers of my book, *Erfahrungen bei Sai Baba in Indien* already know, I changed my life radically at age 40. Thereby I changed the hologram of cancer death, and in fact, the chaotic network of delicate lines in my hand changed into a robust life line.

What is true for the individual life is also true for us as mankind. We co-determine the future of our species and our planet. We shape the future by our being and doing in the present.

In their book, *Mass Dreams of the Future*,[17] Chet Snow and Helen Wambach outline four scenes which 2500 participants of guided inner journeys had dreamed up about the future of mankind and the planet. Four possible holograms are outlined. These are closely connected to the current life styles and experiences of the participants. One describes a sterile space-station world, another is a 'New Age' version of a happy, simple life within a natural environment, the third a technological variant of life in a mechanized, bleak future and the fourth the survival situation after a global disaster.

These scenarios are not an inevitable fate. They are options whose realization depends on what we think, wish and want to create for the future generations here and now. When you consider that the levels of reality unfold and enfold in constant exchange, NOW is the only stage on which you can produce your reality.

If you can influence your future through your thinking, then you can also influence your past. The way you regard your life, your history, is your personal construction of reality. And, as I will point out later, this history is a trap which snares your present and determines your future. It is up to you to decide which events to select and condense into your history.

From therapeutic sessions using the methods of Holographic Analysis, I know that events usually happened quite differently from what is stored in the conscious memory of my clients. The more precisely you see the events as they were, the more you liberate yourself from the bondage of the past. Think about it. It is never too late to make yourself a happy childhood.

---

[17] Chet B. Snow and Helen Wambach: *Mass Dreams of the Future*. New York: McGraw-Hill 1989

## Responsibility

Many people shy away from the thought of taking responsibility for their lives. For them the word is like a red rag to a bull. There are different reasons for this reaction.

### RESPONSIBILITY: GUILT OR FREEDOM?

For some people, responsibility is like a confession of guilt. To say they are responsible means they declare themselves guilty of the pains and the suffering that were inflicted on *them*. In their understanding, that means that the truly guilty can sneak out of their proper responsibility. Therefore, they rebel and generally refuse to take on any responsibility at all.

Others have been told, "You are responsible for that," as if the words were a disciplinary tool. Or they have seen how their parents suffered from the burden of responsibility, or even collapsed under it. Being responsible signifies a ponderous load, one which they are not willing to carry.

For yet others, to be told, "That's your responsibility," was a way of being dismissed when they came asking for support from their parents or friends. This variant is especially popular in esoteric or spiritual circles. Behind the statement is the understanding that a person's outward circumstances reflect their internal reality. The correct application of this principle becomes dubious if it is used as a defense, or an excuse to refuse help.

In its original sense, responsibility refers to our ability to respond appropriately to people, situations and incidents. This presupposes that we are able to recognize what action is appropriate in each moment and that we have the internal freedom to act upon it. According to this understanding, responsibility has much more to do with freedom of choice than with any guilt, burden or imposed external discipline.

Seen in this way, responsibility means that we recognize our life-circumstances as our own creation. Many people perceive themselves as victims of circumstances. They feel at life's mercy and powerless to change their situation.

If I look at the people with whom I work and who share those feelings, I often have to confirm their impression of themselves. They lack both the psychological and physical strength *and* the self-discipline to develop the necessary resources to take charge of their lives. Our comfortable lifestyle is not conducive to strengthening our capacity for stamina and perseverance. And, as I said in the section on addiction to suffering, the subculture of woundology offers sufficient incentives to remain in the suffering state, or to even slip back into the addiction.

## SELF-DISCIPLINE

The term self-discipline has a negative flavor. It is seen as a compulsory exercise or submission to authority, or at least as a restraint on personal freedom. We do not understand that self-discipline is the ability to receive what already belongs to us.

In order to receive, we need a vessel into which the universe can pour its gifts. At the energetic level, this vessel corresponds to your aura or electromagnetic field, on the physical level to your posture and deportment, on the emotional and mental levels to your inner soul dynamics, and on the spiritual level to your connection to other dimensions.

Without the vessel, the energy oozes away like water from a river whose bed has eroded. For most of the people whom I see in my practice, the river bed has unclear contours and holes through which their life-energy drains away. They lack the strength to achieve what they want in their lives. Therefore, they first have to mend the river bed so that it can hold the flow, and then direct it towards the desired goal. This repair work, or perhaps even new construction work, requires daily, disciplined practice.

The difference between external authority and self-discipline is that it is your choice, your responsibility whether or not you undertake this effort. What matters is not what impacted you in your childhood, but what you make out of what happened.

Self-discipline is necessary in order to break with bad habits. We all know how easy it is to establish bad habits and how difficult it is to get rid of them again. Just by analyzing the history of their origins, one does not usually make them disappear. A more effective strategy is to work positive habits into one's program. These positive habits support the building of an inner structure. Implementation of the program requires daily practice and self-discipline.

## THE TRAP OF ONE'S STORY

You need self-discipline to clear up your past. This is easier said than done. Our memory has a tendency to draw together events in such a way that our dignity is guaranteed. And the more frequently we tell our story, the more we are convinced of its truth.

I remember a carved wooden doll which I loved dearly as a child. Relatives from Canada had sent me a "proper" doll, a real treasure in Germany at the beginning of the fifties. She had hair to be combed; she could say "mom," she wore a ball-dress and had an everyday-dress to change into. Yet despite all these advantages, she could not compete with my wooden doll whose body was robust and snug and whose limbs swung at the nails which joined them to the trunk. And most important, I loved her.

One day, this precious doll disappeared and was recalled to memory only thirty years later during my psychoanalysis. Psychoanalysis and therapies in general tend to plough through our lives on their shadow side, searching for memories which can be held responsible for unfulfilled dreams and wishes, for the failure of plans and projects, and one's own deficiencies or life hardships.

And here it was. *The* memory, the quintessential proof of how little my mother had loved me and appreciated and honored my needs. One day, SHE had burnt the doll. Could anything have better expressed her relationship to me than this act of carelessness? And yes! During the psychoanalysis I progressed to the point of counting this as an oversight and not as intended malevolence. It was a step in the direction of forgiveness, but not yet a reconciliation.

One day, when I was preparing to move into the Findhorn community in the northeast of Scotland, my mother brought down a large package from the attic storage and said, "I have kept your toys for you. I thought that it would be lovely for you to have them as mementos." Oh! My whole being shook with painful embarrassment as I rummaged through the box. At the bottom lay the wooden doll. Nothing was left of the splendor which had invested the early childhood days, but she had endured through this long time unharmed.

The shock shattered the story of the rejected daughter, and with it came the collapse of the carefully built card-house of my memories, *my story*. It opened my eyes to what had really happened. However, it took some more years of deep and intense work before I could recognize that the fears and terrors of my childhood had had little to do with my family, that my mother had loved and valued me as much as I could have wished for, and that she and I were just as human as are all mothers and daughters, with our strengths and weaknesses, personal challenges, failures and successes.

This incident stayed in my mind as a warning while I listened to other people tell their story during therapeutic sessions. I knew now how the brain deludes us by selecting and assembling single aspects of events in such a way that it supports our core beliefs. And the more frequently we tell our story to others, the more we are convinced of its truthfulness. I found that to the same degree that I could penetrate the construction of my own story and release it, I could support others in giving up their story.

This is not as simple as it sounds. We are often fundamentally attached to our perception of reality. It gives us identity, it excuses our weaknesses and it justifies our human laziness. Surely, it is the others who are responsible for our suffering! Why then should we strain ourselves to change our life?

To give up our story means taking responsibility for our life, for all that has happened to us, and for all that we have made out of it. To do this, it is often necessary to broaden our perspectives from the level of the personality to that of the soul, which is the higher plan that guides our fate.

## STEPS TO RESPONSIBILITY

To see the events in a new light, you must give up your story. The first step is to trace how *you* produce the events that happen over and over again. This requires some practice, especially when your life's guiding principle is that others are responsible for your suffering.

**Exercise**

➤ As a suggestion, tell your favorite victim story in such a way that you are the producer of the course of events rather than its victim. And instead of complaining that your boyfriends abandon you over and over again, ask yourself, "How do I make a man leave me?" Instead of complaining that your office colleagues gossip about you, ask yourself, "How do I talk about others?" And then observe how this shift in perspective affects you.

The second step is to find out *how* you produce the situations that happen to you over and over again. People tend to evade the answer to this question by making general statements. The devil sits in the details, and particularly in the feelings that are connected to the details. Feelings are the glue that hold together painful and unpleasant memories. We like to bypass them by making general statements.

➤ Fill your story with as many details as possible.

Ask yourself:

▷ *What do the individual phases of this program look like, this one I replay over and over again?*

*What **exactly** hurts me in situations with others?*

*Which words and images emerge over and over again to keep the wound open?*

*Compare several situations in which the same thing seems to have happened.*

▷ *Were the events really the same, or does the watchman in your brain condense different events into the same format?*

*What was different in those situations?*

*What was the 'gift' of each situation? What did you learn from it?*

The third step is to move back into the situations which lie at the root of the 'evil'. In my sessions with clients, I invite their Higher Self to join me. The Higher Self is a bridge between soul and mind and is an expression of the True Self or core of the person. It is closer to the truth than our Ego, for whom it is more important to save face than know the truth.

I ask the Higher Self to lead us back into the situation where we can find the key to the present experience. This key opens the door to what lies underneath the outward symptoms, diseases or problematic life strategies. Such a situation could be a familiar repetitive incident from childhood which now appears in a new light, or a traumatizing experience that has been repressed from consciousness or classified as unimportant.

One such example is the story of a young man who felt that his mother had restricted his spontaneity and vibrant self-expression to the point that he had physical sensations of paralysis and of being crushed. In an inner image, this situation presented itself as a large round stone which had been rolled over a tiger and buried its body. As we looked closer, the stone changed into topsoil which carried a new germ, the germ of a large tree, which was now ready to grow. All the oppressive and constricting forces, which the stone symbolically represented, were at the same time the mother-ground for the unfoldment of his potential.

You cannot recognize this side of the story if you look at it from the perspective of the victim. Only if you put the story into a larger context, if you shift your perspective, can you value the gift that is hidden in it. When you acknowledge and appreciate the positive intent, you can liberate yourself from the entanglements of the past.

In cases where the experiences cut so deeply and were so painful that they are repressed from consciousness, it will take longer to reach their source. You will probably need some guidance, or undertake your own training and practice. Our inner wisdom opens the door to the unconscious only when we are one hundred percent ready to see the truth. A part of the work is just to bring our resistance into conscious awareness. Resistance is another word for fear. Fear has many faces: Fear of the unknown, fear of responsibility, or of being held responsible. We are afraid to change our life and to let go of attachments. And we fear that we will not know who we are without our familiar story.

All these fears are legitimate because they carry a grain of truth. It is important to acknowledge and appreciate them, without getting trapped by them or surrendering our power to them. If we dare to look at them, they lose their power and terror. Upon closer inspection, we find out that underneath the threatening fantasies are events which, seen in the light of day, are human. The knowledge relieves and liberates us.

A child interprets events according to the mental capacities that are available at the time when the traumatic experiences occur. As adults we are more able to accept human limits. To the degree to which we develop understanding and sympathy for our own weaknesses, we can also accept that our parents or the other important people of our childhood were not perfect. At this point we allow ourselves to see the larger truth and say good-bye to our story. At this point we attain the freedom to bring about overdue changes, to dare the new, and to take responsibility for our life.

# Forgiveness

### FORGIVENESS, JUDGMENT AND GUILT

Forgiveness is a word which, like responsibility, is widely misunderstood.

"Forgive your enemy," we learn from the Bible. As a child I thought that meant that you should let people get off the hook. I found that unfair and unjustified.

My native language compounded the difficulty. In German, the same word 'vergeben' is used both for compromising oneself and for forgiving. So to say, "Do not compromise yourself" was like a warning not to forgive yourself. It was like exposing oneself to guilt and shame. So, 'To forgive yourself for something' was obviously an act to avoid. It carried the risk of social disapproval or even ostracism.

I observed that adults who forgave their enemies did so as if acting from a superior standpoint, as if this kind of forgiveness made them a better person. It raised them above those who had inflicted suffering upon them.

I also saw adults who forgave their 'loved ones' in order to avoid any further confrontation. This did not solve the underlying conflict. In the long run, the imbalance brought forth a paralysis or emptiness within the relationship.

I learned that forgiveness was something best avoided.

I was very surprised when later on in life, I read and heard words proclaiming that forgiveness is one key, or even *the* key to happiness. And it took even longer before I could comprehend that forgiveness must mean something different from what I had been taught in my childhood.

Forgiveness within the Christian culture is linked to the concept of guilt. In a culture in which we are accustomed to submit our responsibility to others, we are also accustomed to look for those whom we can blame for all those areas where our success does not meet our expectations. And it is not difficult to find them, be they individual people, superiors, associations, the economy or the government.

This interpretation of forgiveness is based on judgment or even condemnation. Since we are all interconnected, each condemnation also means a self-devaluation. You remember the section about the Holographic Universe? We humans are all tied together. Our thoughts and actions ultimately fall back on ourselves. Each judgment passed on another person speaks as much about ourselves as about the other. Each derogatory judgment about people, events, circumstances and conditions restricts our ability to grow.

If we cease from judging and condemning others, does this mean that forgiveness becomes obsolete?

## FORGIVENESS AND FREEDOM

If you take forgiveness out of the context of guilt and judgment, it changes its meaning. It then becomes what it truly is: a letting go of the past, a bringing home of all those parts of yourself that you gave away to others. It gives you a deeper understanding of the situations that have happened to you.

**Exercise**

▶ Let yourself think about somebody who has done something bad to you, and see how much of your energy is attached to this person.

▷ *How often do you think about this person?*

*What feelings surface if you do so?*

*How far do these thoughts and feelings determine your daily routines?*

*How free are you under such circumstances to control your thoughts and feelings?*

Fury, anger or hate are vigorous drives which direct your life. The more power you give them, the more you draw to yourself situations that reinforce those feelings. This is the law of attraction. It hooks you into a spiral that takes you deeper and deeper into anger, fury and hate.

Forgiveness is the tool to break you free from this negative cycle. By forgiving others, you call back the parts of yourself that you have attached to those people. You can use the retrieved energy to build up your own strength and become whole.

To retrieve your energy, I suggest that you walk a mile in the shoes of the other person and look at the events from their perspective. If you change your viewpoint, the dynamic appears in another light. You receive essential information about the other person which was not accessible from your limited perspective. My clients are often surprised to find out that the action which had hurt them as a child had nothing to do with them personally, but arose from the difficulties and misfortunes of the adult involved.

The father who, out of the blue, verbally attacked his child may then appear as somebody who had just been put down by his boss and subsequently lost his temper on a relatively minor occasion. And the mother who seemingly rejected her child may actually have been battling financial pressures, or was worried about marriage difficulties or a sick brother or sister. The knowledge that one's parents are human, and that they had to cope with the same necessities and challenges which you experience as an adult, reconciles and balances the perspectives left over from childhood.

Forgiveness in this sense means freedom from the chains of the past. Only if you release the past, can you create the space to grow. Forgiveness in this sense means accepting human deficiencies and reconciling with your past. It gives you the option to recognize that the circumstances of your life are your own creation. For this reason, you can change them.

## SELF FORGIVENESS

The most difficult act is to love ourselves. And likewise, it is equally difficult to forgive ourselves. We are often our hardest judges. As we have recounted in the reports about near-death-experiences, the judgments on our lives are not passed by light beings but by the individuals themselves who are confronted by their own feelings of guilt and remorse.

Many people have a little man in their ear who is like a censor and who comments on and judges all impulses and acts. This censor does not allow you any peace. He drives you, criticizes and condemns you. The purpose of self forgiveness is to silence this little man in your ear.

Self forgiveness has nothing to do with atonement. Atonement originates from thinking in terms of guilt. Self forgiveness is an expression of love, and the knowledge that all events are merely a step in our learning process.

This is not a permission to do bad deeds that harm others. Since we are all tied together, since we are all one, each initiative eventually comes back to its source, be it a thought, feeling or action. You are responsible for what you think, feel and do. Whatever you focus on, you multiply. It is up to you whether you multiply the good or the bad.

At times when life seems unjust and unbearable, it may be helpful to look at your soul contract. The soul contract determines our purpose or curriculum for this life. From this perspective we recognize our life's events as steps on the path to self-knowledge. In this understanding, there is no place for guilt or condemnation. Self forgiveness is the natural result of recognizing our path.

**Exercise**

 Let yourself contemplate this point of view, even though it may be unfamiliar to you. And then forgive yourself your deficiencies, your insufficiencies and your failures.

Think of all the people to whom day by day you give away your energy through your negative feelings and thoughts. Make a list of all the people to whom you attach that energy. And then take 15 minutes every day to call back your energy from each person on the list.

If this seems impossible, return to the section on responsibility and write your victim story as if you were the producer.

> ▷ *Why did you produce these painful experiences?*
> *What did your soul want to learn from them?*

If the soul recognizes the message of these events, it liberates itself from the shadows of the past. Your energy returns to you, so that you can use it for your own well-being and the welfare of others.

# Gratitude

## COUNT YOUR BLESSINGS

Gratitude is the key to happiness. In our affluent society we take many privileges for granted. It does not occur to us to be grateful for them. At a seminar, after a meditation on this theme, one woman shared that she had never thought of the fact that first her father and then her husband had provided her with financial security. Instead, she would always think about the things she did not have. And she is not the only one who thinks in that way.

Our cultural attitudes are programmed towards lack, not abundance, towards not-having instead of having, towards deficiencies instead of blessings. It would be healthy for everybody to take account of all the good things in life on a daily basis. Among them are the privileges that are given us by our culture, family membership, profession or personal contacts. We often take them for granted and claim them as our natural birthright.

I well remember my surprise in India when I realized that I had unrestricted entrance to each five-star hotel because of my white skin-color, no matter how I was dressed. With my German passport I can pass most border customs without being exposed to long interrogations or pressure. And the social network allows my parents to grow old in peace and prosperity.

**Exercise**

▶ Take half an hour and write down what you are grateful for in your life.

▷ *Did you have a silver spoon put in your cradle because of your skin color, the culture and society in which you were born, your family membership or the education which was bestowed on you?*

*What have you personally won for yourself that makes you proud?*

*Look around at your job, at where you live, at your family, at your circle of friends? What was given you, what did you achieve by yourself?*

In my seminars I often notice that people seem unable to enjoy the privileges that are their lot as part of an affluent society. Instead, they refer to the costs: the exploitation of the third world or their own emotional misery.

Unquestionably, western wealth has its price which underprivileged people have to pay too. If we recognize that clearly, the logical consequence would be to advocate help for the disadvantaged nations and to increase their prosperity. But that is not how they act, the people who argue with me in this way.

The wealth of the West makes them feel guilty. So they pretend that they are not wealthy. They hide it. Of course, prosperity does not mean only material goods but also inner riches, abilities and strengths, and social and educational opportunities. However, the problem becomes most obvious when we have to deal with bread and butter.

It seems to be part of human nature to believe that things will improve. We cannot imagine that things may get worse. I remember very well my first years at Findhorn. Each year I remarked on New Years Eve, "This was the most difficult year. From now on it can only improve." To my dismay, it did not. On the contrary, it got worse. Underneath the present hell, sheer hell awaited. And, let me add, sheer hell was the turning point. It is a paradox of life that we have to reach the bottom of the valley before we are ready to leave the trodden path and walk another road.

The process is comparable to mountain hikes where one sees one's cottage with welcoming hearth in tangible proximity, and then must walk for many more hours through valleys, round unforeseen detours, and over mountain tops until one reaches it. When I remember such experiences, it makes it easier, even in difficult times, to be grateful that things are not worse.

## MULTIPLY YOUR BLESSINGS

I have said before that gratitude is the key to happiness. Why?

The spiritual laws of the universe teach us that we multiply that on which we focus our attention. If we focus on lack, we produce lack. If we focus on abundance, we produce abundance. Lack and abundance first originate in our thoughts before they manifest in the material world. Whatever we focus on, grows. If we focus on suffering, we multiply suffering. If we focus on joy, we multiply joy.

This principle applies to all areas of life: health, prosperity, relationships or peace. If you are grateful for what you have achieved up to now, you give yourself acknowledgment, appreciation and love.

Remember that present and future are one at this level. If you are grateful for what you are striving for and think of it as already yours, though it still lies in the future, you let the universe know of your firm trust that you will obtain what already belongs to you. The Bible tells us that faith moves mountains. You get what you believe. Gratitude is an acknowledgment of your faith that what you desire is on its way to you. Its appearance on the physical plane is just a question of time.

You say, this is a trick? Yes, it is a trick, but an effective trick because it is in accordance with the universal law. And it is no more or less a trick than the one which you unconsciously use when you continually tell yourself that there is not enough to go round, or that you are not good enough to receive what belongs to you.

Your thoughts determine your reality. Ingratitude means that you focus on what you do not have. In that way you increase the lack.

Ingratitude means that you give more weight to the negative than to the positive. Assume that six people pass by and compliment you, saying how beautiful you look with your new hair style or how much your lecture the other day has helped them. And then comes the seventh and remarks that he finds your new hair style impossible, or else he disparages your lecture. Whose words have more impact? How much weight do you give to the six and how much to the one?

To fail in gratitude is to show a lack of respect and honor for life. If you do not honor and care for what is given you, you shut down the channel through which blessings flow.

The story of my house at Findhorn, which I mentioned in the beginning, provided my own lesson. In my first years there, I lived in a caravan. The roof was full of holes, the floor musty and on top of it all, the oil heater in the kitchen leaked and spoiled the food.

Instead of complaining, I put myself to work and together with the maintenance department, we mended the caravan as completely as possible. I could see that the caravan was providing me with a strong motivation for building a healthy, ecological house, and I gave thanks for it.

After two years, I moved into a room in a house that belonged to the community and found out that wood worm had infested its bearing beams. Together with the house's other inhabitants, we organized the necessary repair work. I ended up spending a good part of my time on a construction site. Instead of complaining, I gave thanks that I had a solid roof over my head and not a draughty trailer.

When this was done, I began the construction of my ecological house. This had its own challenges as you will read later on. However instead of complaining, I gave thanks for the opportunity to practice the laws of manifestation.

Gratitude means that you acknowledge what is given you. It is not important whether this is much or little in comparison to others. It depends on your attitude what you consider much or little. Your starting point does not matter. You can expand and improve your life from each and every point, as long as you are grateful for the opportunities to learn and grow.

To compare yourself to others is the road to ingratitude. Each comparison is based on competition, on winning or losing, being better or worse. Even if you appear to be better than your competitor in one area, you unquestionably will encounter another where your score is worse. And once again, you find yourself dealing with lack, with what you do not have, or are not.

Therefore, be thankful for everything which is given you in your life. It is a way to release the expectations, wants and demands which constrict and limit your potential.

Be grateful for everything that happens. The deeper meaning often reveals itself after the event. Gratitude strengthens one's trust in the goodwill of the universe. This trust is the best safety net in life.


# Service

We are all tied together, we are all ONE. From this perspective all our acts ultimately reflect back upon us. This may be a frightening thought if our life is in a constant chaos. The good news is that the same law holds true for the Good and the Bad. At any time, we have the choice to multiply the Good. Every good deed will benefit us in the end. This is the key and the mystery of service.

### HELPING OR SERVING?

From my own experience, I could not grasp this thought for a long time. To me, service meant duty and responsibility, a burden that made me burn out more than once. I couldn't understand how other people could say that they felt filled with happiness and joy after giving many hours of service.

It was only a few years ago that I learned the difference between helping and serving. When out walking one day, there arose in my heart an urge which was new to me: the urge to give myself, to give my Best and Deepest. This urge was free from all motives of external reward, appreciation or recognition. It was a genuine drive, the pleasure of expressing myself, expanding and sharing who I am.

It was amazingly simple. I didn't have to be or do anything special. It was enough to be. It was enough to express who and what I am here and now. I understood that there is no difference between giving and receiving, that they are truly one. I experienced this physically, as if I were a funnel with two openings. While the energy flowed out from the heart center, the funnel was refilled from the top. Give and take were a circuit that nourished and sustained itself. This giving had nothing to do with exploiting the self, but was freedom, abundance and joy.

Unfortunately such moments do not last forever. They become submerged within the established viewpoints and old habits if we do not make sure that we strengthen them in our daily practice.

And the experience did not correspond to the beliefs that I, and presumably many of you, have grown up with. In my Christian upbringing, service was part of one's duty to be charitable. Through the many years in which I felt obliged to do my duty, I wondered again and again how it could be that I felt burned out and empty after this service. It took many years for me to understand the deeper meaning of the sentence, "Love your neighbor as yourself." I realized that I had not taken into account the second part of the sentence, or else that I had no idea how I could love myself. Deep guilt and shame had taken the place where love should have resided.

For many years of my life, during my twenties and thirties, my work lay in areas of social and emotional misery, with domestic and sexual violence, people in isolation, psychic problems, poverty and disease. And I exhausted my reservoir of strength to the point that I was forced to draw back for a long time just to recover.

I began to suspect that the idea of service needed to be rather different from what I had learned in my Christian upbringing. I saw that many people in the helping professions were motivated as much as I was by their own neediness, helplessness and guilt. Their attempt to help others was an attempt to help themselves. This is a legitimate human motive which bears positive fruit if it is conscious and nourished by the knowledge that we are interconnected. With this insight, we know that everything we do to somebody else, be it good or bad, we do to ourselves.

The Helper Syndrome, as this phenomenon is called in the psychological literature, does not permit this insight. The helper defends himself against his own neediness and helplessness. Instead, he lives those motives through his clients. This collusion, this unconscious contract between the helper and the helped, does not allow the helped to step out of their role and take responsibility for their life.

In our model of service, the relationship between helper and helped looks different. In this case, the helper knows that you do not serve the other by doing their work. A person gains psychic strength and raises his psychic rank by handling his problems himself and refusing to have somebody else to do his work for him. If you cut the cocoon of a caterpillar to help the butterfly emerge, the butterfly dies. Only if the caterpillar frees itself from the cocoon can it change into a butterfly.

In our model of service, you support the other person in finding his own way. If somebody is sitting in a leaking boat, you do not board the boat. You remain standing on the bank, instructing him how to scoop the water out so that the boat arrives safely at the shore and can then be mended. Sometimes, if his boat is already too deep in the water, you must go out with a lifeboat and take the person on board. When you arrive at the shore, you would not then carry that person for the rest of your life, but you would show him how to get back on his own feet. Or would you?

We face the same question on a global level. How can the rich countries best serve the poor countries? In the sixties, this discussion was guided by the principle that it is better to teach people fishing than to bring them fish. The idea here is the same. You keep others in dependence and poverty when you spare them the process which empowers them personally to achieve the results they want.

Of course, there are robust economic interests that determine the approaches nations choose. These are, I suppose, sufficiently clear and well-known. Less clear are the ulterior psychological motives which are fed by the Christian inheritance of guilt and the connection between charity and poverty.

### SHARE AND SERVE

From a Christian point of view, the spiritual path is paired with poverty. Many people who have chosen the spiritual path shy away from money.

One reason is that much of the money on this earth is attended by low motives of greed, personal enrichment and power. People on the spiritual path are afraid to tarnish themselves with money. As long as one feels drawn to any one of these low motives, the fear is legitimate. If one is free of it, one can use money for the welfare of all. And the more you have, the more good you can do.

Another reason is ideological in nature. From a Christian viewpoint, the renunciation of personal wealth is rewarded with inner or heavenly riches. This viewpoint is expressed in the act of charity. To give everything unselfishly and to ask for nothing in return is the path to inner bliss.

It is indeed noble to renounce the material world if one's motive stems from the insight that all we give flows back to us. We are connected with each other. Therefore, we only give to ourselves by giving to others. The taking is contained in the giving.

Renunciation puts on another face if a person reveres poverty because he lacks the confidence to earn money or fears the responsibility of dealing with wealth. This renunciation is no renunciation. It is a lack. We can only renounce what we have.

From our perspective of service, charity has nothing to do with poverty. Service means that you are ready, willing and able to give. You do this by making a positive impact on your own life and supporting others to get what they desire in accordance with the positive laws of the universe. You serve by sharing. You can only share if you have the basic trust that there is enough for everybody, and if you have the freedom to take the share that you need for yourself. If you are at peace with what you are, do and have, you share ungrudgingly.

If you feel however that life neglects and cheats you, you will squint enviously at the things that others have. And in reverse, you will fear the envy and resentment of others as soon as your life gets better. So you will tend to de-emphasize or hide your improved position. No matter whether you are poor or well-off, your constricted viewpoint will prevent you from sharing what you are, do or have.

If you belong to the group of the 'wronged', you may ask, how can I share if I do not have enough?

This is like a dog chasing its own tail. It depends on your viewpoint how much is enough. I know people who have very little money and yet share their meal with their guests; and I know wealthy people where one must ask permission for a glass of water. Not the facts decide the case, but your attitude to the facts. Is the glass half full or half empty? The difference is in your viewpoint.

## THE CORNUCOPIA OF GIVING

If you examine the words of the great teachers of mankind, you learn that the universe is filled with spirit, or light. This spirit or light is limitless, almighty and omniscient. It is abundance, not lack. The 'Nothingness' of the universe is filled with energy, a constant flow of energy. The abundance is a flow of energy.

You as a human being are part of the universe. As such, you are part of the laws of the universe. If you open yourself to its flow, and if you open yourself to both sides of the flow, the giving and the receiving, your life will be enriched inwardly and outwardly. You receive what you can give and take.

The idea that we suffer from lack is a human creation, not the creation of the universe. The problems of poor and rich are problems of distribution, not a question of lack. In order to be part of the flow, you need to understand the laws of the universe and to trust that all that you give will come back to you. You allow this flow to happen when you leave the way open for the universe to respond. Out of uncertainty or an overestimation of our capabilities, we often restrict and limit the ways and means in which we allow the good things to come back to us. If we try to determine them, we limit the possibilities by which the flow returns to us.

I am not talking here about a type of giving that wants something in return and is therefore conditional. I am speaking of the giving that flows inevitably from abundance. This type of giving is service in its genuine sense. Here, giving and taking are inseparably intertwined.

In practical terms this means that if you give love, love will return to you. If you are generous, your life will be filled with inner and outer riches. If you appreciate others in their value and deeds, you will receive recognition and appreciation. Whatever you give to others will return to you. You cannot receive more than you give to others. You harvest what you sow.

## GIVE AND TAKE

For most people, give and take is out of balance. You probably know people who happily give a lot to others, but shy away when they are offered something. Or you can think of people who are always wanting something, or cling on to their possessions out of existential fears. In both cases the flow is interrupted or constricted.

If you restrict your capacity to receive, you either become discontented, or you blame others for their ingratitude, or you burn out. If you hold on to your possessions, you clog up your vessel with old junk. To receive new things, you must empty your vessel regularly. Otherwise, you are in danger of losing your possessions, be they money, people or material objects. You can only keep what you can release.

I suggest two little exercises that will help you to understand the relationship between giving and taking in your inner world.

**Exercise**

▶ Imagine one of the old balance scales with a pan on each side. Determine which side represents giving, which side taking. And then observe how the pans relate to each other. Do they move back and forth, do they find their equilibrium, or is one up and the other down? The one that is down is heavier. In my view this means that the heavier one contains more of my capacities than the lighter one. If the pan of giving moves down, this means that my capacity to give is stronger than my capacity to take.

If the image of the scales does not work for you, you can use instead the physical law which governs communicating tubes. If two tubes are filled with liquid and connected in a U-shape, the level will be the same in both tubes.

▶ Imagine two tubes, one for giving, one for taking. They can be connected at different points such as in a U, or a square, or via a figure 8. They can be different sizes or shapes. This gives you an initial hint how the two sides are developed in you. Just let your imagination move freely.

Determine which side is giving, which side is taking. And then allow your life energy to fill the tubes and watch what happens:

▷ *Are the tubes rather narrow, or are they wide and strong?*

*Are the tubes the same in shape and size or are they different?*

*Does your life energy flow like a river or is it a coagulated mass?*

*How much life force is available to fill the tubes? What height does it reach in the two tubes?*

*Are the tubes connected in a closed system such as a rectangle, or are they instead open like a U? If the shape is a closed one, is the energy circulating through the system or is the flow stagnant?*

Usually, it is easy to interpret the images.

If the flow of energy is too meager to fill the tubes up, refer to the later section  about the Basic Pulsation of Life. In this case, you need to increase your level of energy before you can distribute it.

If one of your vessels is smaller or thinner than the other one, take time to reflect how you could strengthen this neglected side of your life.

If your capacity to give is restricted, can you think of qualities, talents, knowledge or material goods that you might share with others? Refer to the section about gratitude if you cannot think of any area where you can give.

If your capacity to receive is restricted, ask yourself, "What is hindering me from participating with gratitude in the abundance of the universe?" Are you afraid of being obligated? Have you been taught that it is more blessed to give than to receive? Or that it is impolite to reach out for the good things in life and take them?

Be aware that your power to give will decrease considerably if you do not open the funnel that allows you to replenish the vessel.

In the optimal case, you fill up both tubes with your life energy and let it circulate freely through them.

## Finding The True Self

### WHO AM I?

"I cannot find myself." That was one of the things my mother said most frequently after her stroke. It expressed all her pain that she had lost herself and did not know anymore who and where she was.

A stroke is an extreme situation. It tears the brain functions away from their daily routine and it erases memories. However, my mother's words echo a more general theme, that of finding ourselves. The question, 'Who am I?', has engaged me all my life.[18]

You can look at this question by proceeding inversely, by determining who or what you are not. The process starts with the definition of your environment, your family, your school, your friends or, on a larger scale, the mass media which presents you with models with which to identify. We strive to meet these demands until we notice that there is no satisfaction in just living an image.

You can identify with your feelings or your body. You express such an identification when, suffering from a physical disease, you say, "*I am sick.*" In this expression all of you is affected: your thinking, your moods and your ability to act. If instead you used the words, "My body is sick," the "I" would be separate from the body and could still be happy.

Body and mind influence each other. If you know that there is a difference between the two, if indeed you know that the mind can master the body, then "you" impact the physical dis-ease instead of letting the body determine your mood. You influence and shape your life differently, depending on how you answer the question of who you are.

You can also identify with your brain. You probably know the statement by Descartes, "I think, therefore I am." This sentence is correct if we understand the thought process correctly. It is not correct if we restrict the

---

[18] I have extensively described this process in my book: *Erfahrungen bei Sai Baba in Indien*. München: Goldmann 1992. Therefore I refer here to the basic principles.

notion of thinking to the conscious mind. Our actions are largely determined by experiences that we have 'forgotten'.

The statement is also incorrect if we associate thinking only with the analytical part of our brain and set it in contradistinction to feelings. Feeling and thinking are two poles which are both necessary for the understanding of reality.

From brain research we know that our brain has two centers which sort out and apply meaning to the input from the senses. Our left brain is the analytical and our right brain the intuitive part. Both have their specific function in daily life. They supplement each other as a polar unit.

The left brain analyses and reduces events and processes to manageable information and data. It focuses on details and looks for a logical explanation of their connection, while the right brain combines, connects and recognizes the same input in a holistic and analogical way. The left brain is responsible for words, sounds or letters, while the right listens to the melody or the message that sounds or words communicate. It speaks to the feelings and represents the feminine side, while the left half of the brain is the domain of reason. The left side gives an exact meaning to processes and locates them within the space-time continuum. The right places things in a context that goes beyond space and time and thereby speaks to a deeper level of meaning. Dreams and inner images are the material out of which the right brain weaves stories in a metaphoric way, while the left rejoices in mathematical formulae and organized sequences.

The left brain ensures that we cope with our daily routine while the right contains our creative potential. It stands for the artistic and creative element which looks for new possibilities and finds new solutions to old problems. It gives our life intensity and passion, while the left makes sure that we preserve the continuity of our life.

If you want to find wholeness in yourself, you need to have both functions integrated. Our culture over the last two centuries has given supremacy to the rational, logical principle and thereby established traditional science. In the last three decades however, people have recognized more and more that this one-sided focus presents an ecological threat to us as mankind and to our planet.

Many great discoveries are based on intuitive perception, on the divine spark. Jonas Salk developed his vaccine against polio by imagining himself as a polio virus. In this way he grasped its blueprint and purpose. He then identified with the immune system and found out how the immune system could fight the virus.

Einstein confessed many years after his scientific proof of the theory of relativity that he had ridden like a light wave through the ocean of light waves and through this experience comprehended the relationship between light, speed and mass. Only afterwards did he use the analytical function of the left brain to produce the mathematical-logical proof of what had come to him in a dream state.[19]

## THE FOUR WAYS TO PERCEIVE AND PROCESS LIFE

The great Swiss psychoanalyst Carl Gustav Jung provided us with a typology which describes how we perceive and evaluate life. Jung created a matrix out of the two polarities which we use to address problems and orient ourselves in life. Imagine a horizontal axis with 'Sensation' at the left end point and 'Intuition' at the right. A vertical axis crosses the horizontal, and its end points are 'Thought' at the top and 'Feeling' at the bottom. The horizontal line describes how we collect data or receive information, and the vertical how we evaluate them.[20]

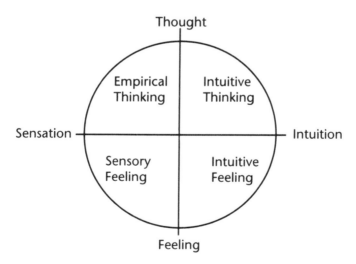

**Figure 2: Jung's Four Functions of Consciousness**

---

[19] Compare Vernon V. Woolf: *Holodynamics*. Tuscon: Harbinger House 1990, p. 59ff

[20] Compare Jolan Jacobi: *The Psychology of C.G.Jung*. London: Kegan Paul et al. 1942

? We use our senses to take in information from the world outside and our intuition to register things from the world within. Our mental capacity evaluates this information from a rational-logical point of view as true or false, while our feelings let us know whether the perception is pleasant or not. Our senses tell us that something exists, our mind tells us what it is, our feelings evaluate whether or not it is agreeable and our intuition tells us where it comes from and where it is going.

Depending on our basic approach to life, we perceive the world predominantly through mental, intuitive, feeling or sensory-perceptive spectacles. To put it differently, we are drawn either to concepts, or the bigger picture, or feelings, or details. If you pay attention to how people use language, you will notice that some usually introduce their sentences with the words, "I think that...," while others say, "I feel that..." or "I sense that..."

Depending on our personal make-up, one of these four functions is the superior one that gets differentiated and refined in the course of life. It acts as a basic tool for orientation and adjustment to reality and is at the disposal of the individual's conscious will. Its opposite end is buried in the shadow side and feels alien and strange. For example, mental people find the reactions of emotional people exaggerated, while emotional people experience the mental ones as cold and callous. Intuitive people perceive the bigger picture and are not interested in details, while sensory-perceptive people love details and combine them to build their understanding of the bigger picture.

The opposite pole to the superior function lies buried in the unconscious and as such does not have the chance to get differentiated through life's experience. It has a raw quality that may break forth from the unconscious when least expected, expressing in an infantile outburst of emotions or judgments. Its threatening quality often gets projected onto the people whose superior function is opposite to ours. They challenge us the most. But if understood properly, they also open the door for us to look at life from a different perspective.

Besides the superior function, people make partial use of a secondary or auxiliary function that is relatively differentiated. It is one of the two that are adjacent to the superior function. If you look at Figure 2, you will see that this may be sensation or intuition for a mental or feeling person; or thought or feeling for a sensory-perceptive or intuitive person.

Empirical thinkers love to use their mental capacity to analyze and look at the details of events. They are drawn to scientific research where they investigate cause and effect in its sequential order. Intuitive thinkers love to look at the bigger picture, drawing up models and concepts of how to develop and enhance current reality. They are the visionaries who have a synthesizing brain that weaves together threads from different sources into a new holistic picture for the future.

Intuitive-feeling people are homebound to their group, where they feel they belong. While the intuitive-mental people use their intuition to grasp whither we are going, intuitive-feeling people look for whence we have come. They look down to the roots that connect us with the earth and the history of our collective evolution.

The fourth group, the sensory-feeling people, work through trial and error. They are impulsive and spontaneous, and enjoy throwing themselves into life, while the empirical thinkers may rather prefer to get some instructions first before they take on the challenge of living through all life's experiences.

Let us take a closer look at the four quadrants or types. Does one of them appeal to you directly? Most people have an innate preference for one of the four quadrants and familiarize themselves with the others later during the course of life. Often the partner represents the antipode, and this helps us integrate this part. Or you may find your counterpart in a work team where somebody represents the particular viewpoint and style which is unfamiliar to you. Our everyday language expresses this phenomenon in the phrase, 'Opposites attract'.

As you look at it, be aware that the function you identify with most may not be the one that is genuinely yours. Most of the people I meet are much more confused about the realms of thought and feeling than about the realms of sensation and intuition. This is mainly due to the high value that is given to the mental-intellectual capacities in our society and the devaluation of the feeling realm.

If you are mainly concerned with naming and conceptualizing your feelings, it does not mean you are a mental person. You are much more likely to be somebody who feels the world and tries to adjust to an intellectual environment. On the other hand, if feelings take up a lot of your mental attention, it does not mean that feeling is your superior function. You are much more likely to be somebody who feels threatened and overwhelmed by feelings and you use your mental capacity to make sense out of them.

If you feel confused at this point, just take a deep breath and leave it alone. During the next days and weeks, just observe yourself leisurely or ask your friends what words you use most: "I think that ...," "I feel that...," "I sense that ...." Those words will point you into the right direction.

Our basic disposition determines the kind of technique or knowledge that appeals to us. Personally, I am most familiar with the intuitive-mental world of the visionary. Therefore it is no accident that I have developed an approach whose main mode is intuition. I will describe it further in the section about Holographic Analysis.

I am also familiar with the other quadrants, having been an empirical researcher and at some points in my life having thrown myself into the midst of events. Sometimes it is the irony of our life path that our social and family situation prevents us from unfolding our strongest side. We are confronted instead by one of the other sides and must first get used to a world that feels alien to us. This happened to me. Only during the years at Findhorn, a community whose main orientation is the intuitive-feeling realm, has my natural channel consciously opened up for me.

The four quadrants inform us about our fundamental way of perceiving and evaluating reality and therefore tell us about our strengths, weaknesses and preferences. They determine how we orient ourselves in society and the job market, which friends and partners we choose, what makes us feel good and what challenges us. They compose the matrix of our personality, the vehicle with which we drive through life.

## THE INNER WISDOM

The vehicle is not the driver. The driver sits behind the steering wheel. You can call him your true self, your higher self, your inner wisdom or your full potential. This true self is part of the universal mind, a drop of water in the ocean or a unique spark in the vast ocean of light.

The inner wisdom is connected with timeless human values such as truth, virtue, peace, love and non-violence. It is at one with the universal mind and works in harmony with the universal laws. It uses the matrix of the personality to express itself, to contribute to life, and create the Positive.

This inner wisdom is a still, small voice which gets lost in the noise of everyday routine if it is not given space to express itself. Many people find it difficult to recognize its voice at all. For me, it took a long time to perceive this voice and to strengthen, refine and differentiate it from the concert of all the other inner voices.

This inner concert is like a radio. You receive from different transmitters on different frequencies and wavelengths. If you take the time to consciously listen to these transmitters you will notice the difference in the quality of their messages. Some transmitters, those which operate on a lower frequency, are full of anger, hate, grief, lust or fear. Others on a higher frequency speak of love, community, abundance or peace. In the short wave and in the middle range where a lot of transmitters overlap, reception often becomes garbled. If you tune your radio to the higher frequencies, your inner voice can come through more clearly.

You can compare this voice to a muscle which you have used rarely or not at all and which therefore has become weak. If you use the muscle regularly, you build up its strength so that it works normally. The same applies to the inner voice. If you set a fixed time for silence, you give yourself a chance to train this muscle. This is the importance of meditation.

The first challenge is to gain access to this voice. To do so, I use an inner journey to the temple of the heart and its temple guide and guardian. In common usage, we associate the heart with our soul attributes. Indeed, the heart is the seat of the soul. The heart is connected to our right brain and our intuition, which together grasp the essence of things without analyzing them.

## THE JOURNEY TO THE INNER WISDOM

For the following journey, set aside half an hour in which you will be undisturbed. Choose a place where you feel safe and comfortable. Use one of the quieter hours of the day, either early in the morning when the hectic activity of the day has not yet started or in the evening when it has finished.

**Exercise**

➤ Assume a posture which allows you to be relaxed and attentive. Many people relax lying down, but there is the danger that you may become inattentive and fall asleep. Others prefer to sit on a chair with folded hands and a straight back while anchoring their feet firmly on the floor. People who meditate a lot often choose the lotus position. It does not matter which position you choose as long as you can relax and follow your journey attentively. Dictate the words – attuned to your own rhythm – on a tape, if reading it would distract you.

▷ *Imagine that a balloon with a basket lands next to you... You board the basket, the balloon rises into the air and carries you over a landscape...*

*Look at the landscape. How does it appeal to you? How do you feel?...*

*The balloon glides evenly through the air, and you become quieter and quieter in yourself as you look at the landscape...*

*Slowly the balloon begins to sink, and the basket comes to earth at the beginning of a path...*

*You step out of the basket and walk along the path...*

*There are flowers along the path. Now and then you stand still and smell a flower...*

▷ *You come around a bend and see a lake in front of you. On the other side there is a temple...*

*What is your impression of the temple from a distance?... What does it look like?...*

*How do you feel about it?...*

▷ *You go to the shore and test the water with your toes. It is pleasantly warm...*

*You take off your clothes, get into the water and swim or walk to the other side...*

*On the other side, clothes have been laid out for you. Look at them. How do they look?...*

*What material are they made from?...*

*What color are they?...*

*How do they feel?...*

▷ *You put the clothes on and go to the temple. Walk around the temple. How does the temple affect you now?...*

*How big is it?...*

*Of what material is it constructed?...*

*What color is it?...*

*Is the temple well preserved, or has it fallen in, or have any areas become ruined?...*

*Is it a temple which appeals to you?...*


▷ *See if there is an opening through which you can enter the temple...*

*Go inside...*

*What does the temple look like from within? Is there one room or several?...*

*Do you feel surprised because you had expected something else?...*

*If there are several rooms, go into the main one. Here you will meet the temple guardian...*

*Look around you. Are there seats, or would it be more appropriate to stand in a particular place while waiting for him. Take your place there...*


▷ *Breathe deeply and let go of all thoughts...*

*Now you sense that somebody is in the room with you. It is the temple guardian. Do you feel his presence without seeing him?...*

*Or does your temple guardian have a visible form?...*

*Is it a human figure?...*

*An animal or a fabulous creature?...*

*A figure from another dimension like a light being, an angel or a fairy?...*

*A color or a geometric figure like a circle, ball or triangle?...*

Be open. The temple guardian can take many shapes. Pay attention to how you feel about the temple guardian. Does his presence fill you with trust? Do you feel safe, even at home, in his presence?...

▷ Feel his presence and see whether the temple guardian has a message for you. This message can come in words, images, body sensations or as an inner knowing...

You can also ask the temple guardian a question, one to which you have always wanted an answer...

Be open to his message, no matter in what way it gets transmitted...

▷ Your time with the temple guardian comes to an end. Before you take your leave, ask him whether you may return to the temple whenever you need advice and support...

Ask him whether it would be a good idea to arrange a regular time to strengthen the contact...

Now you say goodbye and return to the shore of the lake...

▷ You take off your clothes, swim or walk back through the lake and put on your regular clothes...

You go back along the path to the balloon, climb into the basket and allow yourself to be carried back through the air to your point of departure....

Take the time to write down the essential features of the temple. The temple symbolizes your heart. How does it look from a distance, from near by, from within?...

▷ Who is your temple guardian?...

Is he part of a particular tradition or does he come from another dimension?...

How do you feel about this inner guide?...

What was his message for you?...

*Can you imagine working together with him on a regular basis?...*

*Are you ready to commit yourself to a regular appointment?...*

▷ *Examine the clothes you wore. Which style, what color expresses your innermost being?...*

Your inner images impart hints about traditions which may be close to your heart. A path that is already known to your innermost being is easier to walk down than a completely new path.

## THE EVOLUTION OF THE SELF

Like a pomegranate which waits for the opportunity to unfold its abundant potential, your inner core contains many seeds. It is up to you which seeds you want to nurture and tend.

The Bible teaches us that we harvest what we sow. If we sow love, we harvest love. If we sow hate, we harvest hate. Choose carefully which seeds you want to bring to harvest.

In each seed there is a potential enfolded that awaits its evolution. The first step is to recognize this enfolded potential and help it to sprout by giving it the right amount of energy and attention.

Due to your childhood experiences, some seeds may have developed into sprouts, or even plants, which are immature or disturbed and do not serve their life configuration. You need to help these sprouts mature by recognizing their positive intent and then preserving them in a higher order.

Learn to concentrate and direct your physical and inner power; to use resources appropriately; and to work together with those people who support your goals. In this way you create the space and conditions through which your nature can unfold and express its full potential.

I present strategies for this process in the sections on Growth and Transformation.

# Growth

## GROWTH AS A PRINCIPLE OF LIFE

Life is growth. Growth is change and flow. The Greek philosopher Heraclitus coined the saying that we never step twice in the same river. The only constant in the universe is change: movement, expansion and evolution to higher and more complex forms of consciousness. Creation is an unfolding process that happens in each moment. As part of creation, you cannot escape this process. You can only decide whether to grow more quickly or more slowly. That will depend on whether you swim with the flow or against the flow. You can suffer through the process by digging in your heels against the flow, or you can go with it and grow through joy.

Going with the flow means that you say goodbye to certainties, habits, convictions and behaviors which no longer serve you, and that you open yourself to what truly belongs to you and thereby accept it. Going with the flow means that you do not perceive obstacles as barriers blocking your way, but as signposts pointing out what you need to change in your life and what direction to take.

Life is not a linear process, nor is growth. It is more like a pendulum which swings from one side to the other within an overall upward movement. This movement corresponds to the polarity of the basic rhythms of life, such as inhale and exhale, or contraction and expansion in an ascending direction. In the 19th century, the German philosopher Hegel summed this process up in the concept of the dialectic. Each thesis generates its antithesis which will then integrate on a higher order to a new synthesis. This new synthesis again generates its own antithesis and this integrates on the next higher plane to another synthesis.

Nature knows this process as mutations, quantum leaps from which new forms suddenly emerge. Growth in nature is the reorganization of simple, repetitive patterns on a higher plane of complexity. A characteristic of this process is that things which previously opposed each other as irreconcilable opposites, in this higher context coexist in simultaneous synthesis.

In my practice I often meet with people who are enmeshed in a separation conflict with a partner. They come to me with the question, "Should I stay or leave?" Whatever they decide, their problem is rarely solved. If they move apart and occupy two different spaces, they stay inwardly connected. If they stay together, they inwardly strive to be apart. The solution does not belong on this level since in such constellations each of the possible solutions keeps the partners unhappily attached. I usually tell them, "Separate while staying, and stay while separating."

I then explain that the question is not at all concerned with moving apart on the outer, but with an inner separation and differentiation. Only when the inner maturation process allows both to stop seeing the other merely as a part of themselves, can they start to see the other in his or her own right. Then the question arises, what would they like to do with each other in the future? Whatever the chosen solution looks like, it represents a higher order of relationship than the previously described Either-Or situation.

Every time you grow, you change. In most people, each change brings out resistance. You may know the story of the man who was fed up with carrying his cross around. He went to a shop which had many different crosses in its stock, and offered his cross in exchange.

"That's okay", said the shopkeeper, "Just look around and select a new one." He walked around and tried many crosses. One pressed here, another pressed there, one was too heavy, the next too thin, the third too worn, the fourth too new. After a long search he finally found a cross that was tailor-made. Glowing, he went to the shopkeeper.

"I'll take that one", he said happily.

The shopkeeper agreed, nodding his head. "This is the cross you came in with."

Are you ready to say goodbye to your cross? And not only to your cross, but to crosses in general? Can you imagine that people actually live without a cross and enjoy their lives? Living without a cross means that you make decisions. You choose, even if you are not conscious of your choice. Carrying your cross is as much your choice as the decision to live without. The cross in the Christian tradition stands for suffering. As I pointed out in the section about 'Heaven and Hell', you can also view the cross as a transition into a higher order of life, into resurrection or oneness with the universal mind that brings joy, abundance and fulfillment to your life. Which do you choose? Joy or suffering?

## Table 1: The Six Stages of Development

| I | II | III | IV | V | VI |
|---|---|---|---|---|---|
| **Physical Well-Being** | **Personal Well-Being** | **Interpersonal Well-Being** | **Social Well-Being** | **Principled Well-Being** | **Universal Well-Being** |
| Vitality | Creativity | Intimacy | Synergy | Integrity | Oneness |
| Abundance | Confidence | Friendship | Teamwork | "I am" | Knowing |
| Health | Self-assertion | "We are okay" | Open trust | Owning it | Empowered |
| Strength | "I am okay" | Mutual respect | Comradery | Fair-care-share | Loving |
| Energy | Self-discovery | Rapport | Cooperation | Openness | Attuned |
| **CHOOSE** To live / Not to live | **CHOOSE** To unfold / Not to unfold | **CHOOSE** To commit / Not to commit | **CHOOSE** To act / Not to act | **CHOOSE** To become / Not to become | **CHOOSE** To extend / Not to extend |
| Deprivation | Denial | Disconnected | Conformist | Rationaliser | Detached |
| "Dingbat-role" | Fear | Manipulator | "Shoulds" | Pretentious | Remote |
| Dis-ease | Anger | "Match-my-images" | Rule-bound | Hypocrite | Aggrandised |
| Zero power | Insecurity | Pleaser | Role-bound | Unethical | Obsessed |
| Shut down | Self-defeating | Victim | Judger | Unscrupulous | Tyrannical |
| **Physical Disorder** | **Personal Disorder** | **Interpersonal Disorder** | **Social Disorder** | **Principled Disorder** | **Universal Disorder** |

*Printed with kind permission of the author*

Source: V. Vernon Woolf: *Holodynamics*. Tuscon: Harbinger 1990 S.48

## CHOICES

Growth is the gradual development of qualities and values. You can jump stages, but that usually causes pain, torment, and in the main, failure.

At each stage you are confronted with a choice. You decide whether you want to expand or constrict yourself. If you choose expansion, you explore at each stage the manner in which you want to realize its potential in your daily life. When you have gained sufficient experience and have overcome the challenges of one stage, you proceed to the next higher one and start on the next cycle of gaining wisdom and experience.

In his book, *Holodynamics*, Vernon Woolf distinguishes six stages, each of which we explore, master and leave behind as we grow and unfold our potential.[21]

In the first stage, we become aware of our physical environment. Here we learn to deal with the material world. We take care of our body and our health. Before we do this however, we need to decide to be in this world as physical beings. This is not to be taken for granted. Choosing to live here means that we are investing our life vitality in a certain potential.

If you choose not to, you withdraw your life energy. You feel switched off, have zero power and feel neglected by life or generally uncomfortable with yourself.

In the second stage, you become aware of your identity as a person. You become an "I". You become aware of your thoughts and feelings and you gain self-confidence. When you have made the decision to invest your energy in the material world, you then decide whether or not you want to unfold your potential here.

If you answer 'Yes' to yourself, you start on an inward journey of discovery to your inner core. You unfold your creativity based on the notion that you are okay. If however you decide against the evolution of your potential, you get stuck in fears, uncertainties, denials or self-defense.

In the third stage, the consciousness recognizes other people as other "selves" and starts to relate to them. At this stage we develop mutual respect, trust and friendship. We embark on the risky journey of intimacy,

---

[21] There are many different models which describe the growth process. Many may know Abraham Maslow's model from the psychological literature. Ken Wilber outlined the process from a system point of view. I had good experiences in my practical work with Vernon Woolf's model.

sharing our deep feelings, yearnings and vulnerability with others. We discover how it feels to become part of another person's life.

At this stage, the choice is your willingness to fully commit yourself to another person or a task. In a relationship, this means loyalty to the partner and the willingness to maintain the relationship through all hurdles. At work, it means a commitment to complete, in spite of all difficulties, the task which you have taken on.

If you shy away from this openness and commitment, you risk becoming isolated, or you may try to manipulate people and events in your own interest. If the manipulation does not succeed, you may feel as if you are a victim of circumstances.

In the fourth stage, the consciousness expands to 'systemic thinking'. We recognize that we are part of larger systems: neighborhoods, circles of friends, organizations or nations. Here we learn to work together in open trust and teamwork with people beyond our familiar world.

Here, the specific question is whether you act in harmony with your own commitments or not. If you decide to commit yourself to a project, the consequences are given. It is up to you now to deal responsibly with those consequences. This can mean that you collect information and make it available; that you directly confront and resolve conflicts with other team members instead of gossiping behind their backs; or else get support from outside if you cannot resolve a team conflict yourself.

If you are not ready to take over the responsibility for your actions, you may hide behind social rules and regulations. You fulfill the roles that are attributed to you and condemn all those that do not conform.

In the fifth stage, the consciousness comes to understand and to identify with the principles by which systems live and grow. Here you learn about love and trust, truth and honesty, compassion and integrity. You learn to live these principles, to become them.

To become these principles means that you integrate them into all levels of your being. At this stage for example, you know that you are responsible for your life.

If you refuse the responsibility, if you decide not to integrate your current experiences, you risk rationalizing your actions. This can mean that you say one thing and do another. You keep up a good appearance and behind it you unscrupulously pursue your own interests.

### Table 2: Needy and Mature Love

| Stage | Needy and Dependent Love | Mature Love |
|---|---|---|
| **I Physical and material world** | Refusal of sex<br>Sex-addiction and sexual dependency | Sexuality as an expression of intimacy |
| **II Personal level** | Self-devaluation<br>Identity as someone who searches for love | Self-appreciation<br>Self-fulfillment<br>Self-love |
| **III Interpersonal level** | Romantic love<br>Relationship addiction<br>Co-dependency<br>Symbiosis | Intimacy<br>Commitment<br>Bringing out the best in the other person |
| **IV Social level** | Helper-organization<br>Community as escape from intimacy<br>Competition for attention<br>Holding on to status | Cooperation<br>Team spirit<br>Care<br>Focus on common good<br>Free flow of energy<br>Freely moving hierarchy |
| **V Principles** | Abuse | I am Love<br>Love expresses itself through me |
| **VI Universal level** | Despotism | Unconditional love<br>Universal love |

If the consciousness understands the principles on which all systems live, it naturally applies them to all people. This means that you not only love your neighbors, but that all are your neighbors. At this sixth, universal stage you are conscious of your inner connection with all life. Your being radiates and manifests the principles of love, trust or compassion as its natural characteristics in your relationships with others.

If you decide to expand in this sense, it becomes an inner need to realize your life purpose. You keep your commitments, see projects through all difficulties, process your experiences and integrate them into your being. In this way you realize your full potential.

If however you decide at this stage to withdraw your energy, you run the risk of overvaluing yourself: perhaps becoming an elitist who turns away from others as someone 'better' than they; or trying tyrannically to dominate over others.

In the course of life we traverse through the stages over and over again, just as long as we move along making positive and negative choices. You may find yourself at several stages simultaneously. You take care of your physical needs and emotional well-being, you learn in relationships, you are a part of groups or systems, and you ponder the values that you would like to guide your life. In this sense, it may look as if all stages are equivalent.

If you look closer, you will notice however that the stages build on each other like the steps of a spiral staircase. The more thoroughly and more consciously you pass through each stage and complete it, the more strength you gain from the process for a positive and powerful approach to the next stage. I will use the process of love to elaborate this point further.

## LOVE AS A GROWTH PROCESS

Love is the power which holds the universe together. Love takes its place with wealth and health as the three topmost desires for which most people strive. Your understanding of love depends on the stage from which you basically run your life.

At the stage of physical well-being, love is the satisfaction of vital sensual needs and the expression of physical pleasure and vitality on the basis of an intimate connection.

If this physical well-being is disturbed, you may refuse sexual contact, or it may turn into sex addiction and sexual dependency. You can then only see the other as an object who will satisfy your needs. In sex addiction you satisfy your need for stimulation, in sexual dependency your need for affection.

At the stage of personal well-being, you care for what is the best for you and what will fulfill you. What's important at this stage is to accept and love yourself exactly as you are, with all your strengths and weaknesses. Self-Love in its positive quality allows you to feel whole and complete, so that you do not need another person to boost your self-esteem. On the contrary, you give love out of your abundance instead of expecting it from others.

If this personal well-being is disturbed, if you do not know or acknowledge your own value, you make yourself dependent on the appreciation and love of others. You need others to replenish yourself. Instead of looking for sexual approval as in the physical domain, you require appreciation, identity and self-confidence at the emotional-mental level. You think of yourself as somebody who needs love, not as somebody who can give love. The needy type of love can disguise itself as a source that thinks itself inexhaustible but very quickly consumes itself in giving. That is the difference between it and the true inexhaustible source of love which enriches you.

At the interpersonal stage you look for somebody who supplements you, stabilizes you in your self-esteem and satisfies your needs. According to the law of attraction you will seek out someone who looks for the same things. The dilemma is that two dependent people, who find each other because of their neediness, are not in a position to fulfill the needs of the other. They cling together like two burdocks without being able to give each other the nurturing that each of them needs so badly. The frustration arising from the lack of fulfillment leads to anger and hate. Some play this game of love and hate for the rest of their lives. Others quit and move on in search of a better substitute. If you refuse to unfold your potential, the replacement strategy usually ends in the same disaster.

If you know your own worth, you recognize the worth of others and you accept them. Since you are self-sustained, the other does not need to change in order to fulfill your needs. On the contrary, you support him or her in unfolding their own potential. You stand back, or if necessary, you step in on their behalf. You openly share your strengths and weaknesses, expose your vulnerability and deepen the intimacy of the relationship.

To say 'yes' to an intimate partner is a commitment that provides the needed security to jointly endure and work through crisis situations. The relationship is an instrument of growth, and growth signifies that you will move and progress at different speeds at different times. These imbalances however do not put the relationship at risk. They rather release the potential for creative solutions.

The ability to engage in an intimate encounter, to have an open and honest dispute, is the core condition for cooperation in larger circles of people. From the seed of the pair relationship or family, one's awareness on the social level expands to the social orders which guarantee the well-being of all. Through your abilities, your dedication or your love, you strengthen your neighborhood, your job or the organizations which you have joined. You work together with others on goals which serve the preservation of life and the Common Good.

Since you are able to make a stand for your values and goals, you are able to engage in teamwork and cooperation or make decisions on your own if necessary. At this stage you understand the principle of synergy, this 'extra' of power and spirit which joins the individual interests and at the same time transcends them. Synergy means that you use your strengths for the good of all, and at the same time you are carried by its power. At this stage you make sure that community resources are used appropriately and that decisions are made by those who know the issues at hand and not through the process of a bureaucratic hierarchy. You flow with what needs to unfold, you do what is necessary and you get rid of all that is unusable. You create the new and serve life in its larger contexts.

On the other hand, if love means to you that others should mother and protect you, you may at this social level of development look for a community that will fulfill these needs. This is even more likely if you have not succeeded in satisfying these needs within a couple relationship. The community becomes a mother substitute. If the community is mainly composed of individuals with the same interests, you will not find synergy. Instead there will be battles for attention, a lack of respect for other members, concealed and hidden power struggles, an orientation towards outside models and an earnest attachment to whatever privileges have been acquired.

The romantic love of the couple relationship shifts to an idealized community ideology. That ideal is as impossible to reach as is the romantic ideal of love and leads to as many frustrations and disappointments. One's own unresolved neediness shifts into the helper syndrome symptomatic of many helper organizations and spiritual communities. And since helping stems from lack, it leads to burn-out instead of enrichment. This applies to the single person as well as to the group.

At the stage of principles, we usually begin to comprehend these connections. Here you start to recognize the dynamic that results from a lack of love, with all its consequences on the physical, personal, interpersonal and social levels. Lack generates lack. As long as see yourself as somebody who 'needs' love, the need will stay unfulfilled on all four levels. It will return only when you begin to give love instead of demanding it. The key to this is the shift from helping to service.

Helping takes the position that it is superior. Service is humility. By serving others you transcend the needy position which stares at its own navel. The first step may be to love yourself, to make yourself into a channel through which the positive energy can flow. This center of being love differs from wanting love. If you are love, love expresses itself through you and returns to you. The key is the evolution of your own potential.

Once you have recognized the dynamic of a 'needy' love, you can choose to walk simultaneously on two paths: love for yourself in its positive sense, and service. Both are inseparably interrelated. In practice this means that you use the knowledge of the fifth stage to consciously pass once more through all the stages of development. You fill each stage with a mature expression of love. You will then recognize what hinders you from radiating love at each stage and find ways to overcome these obstacles.

When you integrate all that you have learned in all the stages, you become an embodiment of love that of itself reaches out to all people. This feeling of universal love is the expansive feeling of compassion of which Buddha spoke. It is the wish to ease suffering, and by pointing out the transitory nature of this world, ultimately show the people the way out of suffering. If you strive to attain this stage coming from the needy position of love, you may easily fall back into the romantic and illusory assumption that you only need to proclaim unity in order to manifest it. Then you do not realize where the world is at, and you do not develop the ability to react appropriately to it.

### CHALLENGES

Each stage has its own qualities and challenges. Although they build on each other, they are at the same time interwoven in such a way that you need the experience of the higher planes to solve the challenges of the lower planes. Imagine that the passage through the stages of development is like walking up a spiral staircase. You pass by the same walls in many winding circles. Each time you pass by the same 'stones' of the wall, you integrate them into your current experiences on a higher plane. This means that you return again and again to the physical plane and pass through the same stages of development, but with more experience, understanding, consciousness and creativity.[22]

The stages have different degrees of difficulty. The first two, the physical and personal planes, usually take the longest time. The process is like that of the small child who takes a lot of effort and trouble to learn to sit, crawl and walk before he gains the freedom to explore his environment.

---

[22] Compare the next section about the 'spiral staircase' (page 102) for a deeper understanding of the cyclic nature of life

The challenge in mastering these planes is to find the right balance between 'too little' and 'too much', the healthy middle ground, the YES to life in all its functions and shapes. And like the autopilot in an airplane, we find the right course by veering away from the center line in many little deviations back and forth.

## THE YES TO LIFE

People think that just the bare fact of their bodily presence on earth is already proof that they consent to physical existence. However, for me, my work with people on the spiritual path is a constant reminder of what an effort it can be to engage in the material realm of life.

The body with all its uncontrollable impulses appears to those people like a prison from which they escape by withdrawing from material things. They create their own inner world which protects them from the 'dirt' or the 'temptations' of the physical, and more specifically, the sexual impulses.

Not just the body seems an affliction, but also all the other demands of physical existence like money, living space, food or sporting activities which keep the body healthy and vital. Rejecting the material world, they find it difficult to make their physical existence secure, let alone make themselves at home here. They restrict themselves to the bare necessities and justify their inability to deal with material requirements by placing emphasis on human and mental values.

On the other hand, we find other people with too strong an attachment to the physical world, people nurtured by the illusion that the material world will fulfill all their needs. Money and sexuality are the predominant drives which attract these people. Money promises fulfillment on the outer, sex fulfillment on the inner planes. Unfortunately, both can only be a substitute for one's need for a deeper meaning in life, or in human contacts and connections. If they are not tied into a higher order, they will leave you feeling more and more dissatisfied and empty.

Material goods or sex cannot give you that deep connection with life which brings peace and stillness to the human being. Instead it just washes over the inward emptiness, increasing the discrepancy between the inner yearning and the potential for its fulfillment. On the physical plane, more and more refined delights beckon towards the illusory fulfillment of that which can first be attained only on the plane of the principles, your inner connection with the life-enhancing qualities.

To search in the wrong place necessarily leads to frustration and feelings of failure. If you do not recognize this, you run the risk of thinking that you, your partner or your circumstances are not good enough. So you try 'more of the same', until the search condenses into an addiction to material or sexual fulfillment. This path can be so disappointing and disheartening that the only way out may seem to be a radical withdrawal from the material world, in other words, suicide.

The YES to life means the application of practical reason: the healthy middle ground between escape from earthly gravity and the demands of the material world on the one hand, and on the other the unrealizable promises of material happiness or satisfaction in mere sex.

The YES to life means the commitment to maintain and improve life. If you say YES to life, you express your willingness to take care of your physical existence. You are willing to learn how to get what is needful for your daily living without wasting unnecessary time. You are aware of the limited span of life and the preciousness of the present moment. Therefore you use your time. Your goals are attuned to your values, and you pursue them consistently.

The YES to life, the YES to physical existence, presupposes that you are aware of the preciousness of life. You understand that the body is the temple of the soul and that the body is a necessary and irreplaceable vehicle for this life. So you need to take good care of it. You do what is needed to keep your body healthy and vital so that you have the stamina and strength to realize your goals. This can mean that you commit yourself to learning all that is needed for your health and to uniting all aspects of your personality behind this objective.

The unrestricted YES to life means that you are aware of the creative power of the sexual energy. In a culture which reduces sexuality to a pretty label on merchandise and to intercourse and the discharge of semen, it is not easy to remember this knowledge, or even to find out about it.

Many people, especially of the younger generation, have grown up with the understanding that sexuality means sensual stimulation or excitement through outward attractiveness. Women get programmed by the media to become the seductive and always eager sex symbol in charming underwear, sheer stockings and with perfect body. Men are told to become the strong and always potent man.

Considering our everyday reality, these demands bring about such fears of failure that both genders may be reluctant to engage in this area. In consequence, we are unfamiliar with sexuality as an expression of the basic energy of life, as a creative power that produces life on all levels. A satisfactory sexuality is the expression of a deep connection as well as a pleasurable and creative act that, used consciously, can help two partners create a common ground. In practice, this can mean that both agree before making love who or what in their life should profit from the loving energy of the union.

A satisfactory sexuality grows when you feel connected on a deep level with the other person and simultaneously you stand on your own ground and maintain your own point of view. Each person has their own basic rhythm which becomes especially noticeable in the sexual area. You not only need to know and own your own rhythm, but at the same time adjust to the rhythm of the other person.

The first requirement is that the biological and emotional rhythms should fundamentally agree. The old cultures were aware of the importance of this harmony and checked astrologically to determine which partners would blend emotionally and physically. In our culture, which assigns much more meaning to romantic love than to the harmony of bodies and souls, the incompatibility of many partners' rhythms creates much grief. Even therapeutic efforts can hardly resolve such a fundamental, biological difference.

If your rhythms are fundamentally in accord with your partner's, there will still be periods in life when your partner's or your own energy are otherwise used up. This is the case for example in times of young motherhood, stress, loss of close friends, financial worries or sickness. In such times it is important to know your own needs and to share them openly and frankly. It will be easier to do this if you have unfolded your personal self in such a way that you can say YES to yourself.

### THE YES TO THE SELF

In saying the YES to the self, the first hurdle to overcome is your own image of yourself. Your environment tells you to see yourself in a certain way or to fit a certain image. As parents, you pass on your unfulfilled desires and expectations to your children in just the same way that your parents bequeathed their unfulfilled wishes and expectations to you. You are part of the generation chain and bound to traditions whose roots reach deeply into the unconscious and are not so easily detected. On top of it all, the prototypes in the media approve and establish such programming.

The second hurdle lies in the programming set up by the idea of the 'Either-Or', the too little or too much, the victim or doer, the self-devaluation or grandiosity. "Who am I to..." is one side of the medal, "If they only knew who I really am..." is the other. If this 'pair' doesn't ring a bell with you, try, "Who are you to..." and "If they only knew who I really am..."

Both sides are inseparably linked.. The devalued child cures the injury to the self by making him or herself bigger than the others. This 'making bigger' often arises out of a feeling of revenge which says, "One day I will show you...". The motive for revenge together with the power that flows from it can become an essential motor for outward success.

The dilemma facing this attitude is that the outer strength covers the fragility of self-devaluation. Whoever devalues himself needs to prove himself over and over again. If the proof should fail, the self-devaluation breaks forth again and embitters one's life with all its shadow sides of guilt, shame and failure.

To get out of this dilemma you need to break free of the cycle of self devaluation and grandiosity. In most cases, you are neither so little nor so big as you, in your inner carrousel, believe yourself to be. It helps my clients to realize that they are human and are limited in what they can achieve and cope with, and conversely that they can demand more of themselves than they would like to believe from a position of self devaluation.

The overweening or grandiose self cannot bear to make mistakes. It must be perfect immediately. It does not allow you the delight of searching, learning through trial and error, and exploring boundaries. The grandiose self prevents you from taking a look at yourself honestly because you might discover a flaw. For the perfect self, a flaw is an injury. A flaw suggests that the self is perhaps not as grandiose as it needs to be to compensate for the devaluation.

If you can admit to yourself that you are in this school 'Earth' just because you are not perfect, just because you have to master learning tasks, then this knowledge can be a great relief. Take as an example the needy love which we discussed in the last section. The needy love is neither good nor bad. It is a learning experience which derives from an actual defect in childhood. As an adult, you have the chance to give your inner child the nourishment which your parents or relatives were not able to give because of their own life history. With that, you break loose from the generation chain and prepare a new ground in which you set the seed of self-fulfillment, self-appreciation and self-love.

I meet quite a few people who refuse to take care of their inner child until they have obtained similar nourishment from another person. They refuse to love themselves as long as they do not feel loved by somebody else. They are stuck on the stubborn notion that the world owes them something, or that they do not have enough to give to themselves.

This is the dilemma. You cannot utilize the love nourishment of another person if you have not prepared your own inner ground. If this ground is not made ready, all that comes from outside oozes away and leaves you with the feeling that there is not enough for you, while your 'nourisher' gets the feeling that you are insatiable. And the dilemma is that both of you are right.

You prepare the inner ground by nourishing yourself. There are several ways to do this. You can get in touch with your inner child and through a silent dialogue find out what needs remain unsatisfied. There is a broad spectrum of unsatisfied life needs arising out of childhood. There is the physical need to be protected from harm and to be nourished by life-giving food; the self-need to be seen and appreciated; and the social need to playfully explore the environment, knowing that you can return to the 'motherly' source for comfort and bonding.

Many of these needs you can satisfy by using your caring grown-up self to your advantage. If you have the impression that your grown-up self is still too needy herself to be able to nourish the inner child, turn to the temple guardian whom I introduced in the last section, or else see whether you have a motherly inner figure who would fulfill the needs of your inner child today.[23]

In this way your organism learns to receive and digest life-giving food. People who are able to receive such and take it in need surprisingly little from outside. In farming vernacular, they are good 'doers', metabolize well and are content with little. At the same time, they are also the ones who draw affection, attention and love to themselves. It is a paradox of life that those who have, get more.

---

[23] Compare: 'The Journey to the Inner Wisdom' in the last section and 'The Inner Guide' in the section about Transformation

## THE **YES** TO THE OTHER PERSON

Many couples come together as if with the motto that it is better to be alone with two than alone with one. They see the other person as a part of or an extension of their own selves. This means that the other has value and meaning only in so far as he/she can fill the gaps in one's own system. Our everyday speech expresses this well-known state of affairs with the term, 'better half'.

Originally, this idea referred to the economic and social distribution of roles and obligations between men and women. Both had different functions within the bourgeois society. The men took care of the financial needs of the family while the women looked after the upbringing of the children. To the degree that these functions were taken over by both sexes, the distribution of tasks and obligations became an inner rather than an outer reality.

On the inner stage, people look for somebody who promises to provide that wholeness that they cannot give themselves. The ideal of romantic love beguiles people into believing that there is a prince on a white horse who will awaken the sleeping beauty with his kiss. Or that there exists the eternal feminine who will bring to the man the fulfillment of his dreams.

In the media, the hit industry hammers the savior-motive into our brains as a reality ("and then he/she came..."). The theme addresses deep-seated needs in each one of us and it is not so easy to escape its grip. In the light of the promised possibilities, no partner can be good enough for the needy self as long as the needy self is not good enough for itself. And the rather arduous method of building trust, reliability and commitment appears a laborious undertaking in comparison to the 'instant' happiness which is promised if one only waits long enough.

Relationships today are a central instrument for one's own growth. Gregg Braden[24] calls them the modern temples of Initiation. As in the Egyptian temples of Initiation where people went to confront themselves and overcome their shadow sides, relationships today confront people with their unfulfilled longings and the resulting feelings of disappointment, jealousy, envy, revenge and anger. Depending on how consciously you deal with it, the partner is either the projection screen for your unsatisfied and unfinished shadow side, or a mirror in which you can recognize yourself.

---

[24] Gregg Braden: *Awakening to Zero Point. The Collective Initiation.* Sacred Spaces/Ancient Wisdom. Mexico 1994

To live a fulfilled partnership in mutual respect and freedom is nowadays an art at which not many succeed. The old forms are dissolving and new ones have not yet developed to be learning models or guidelines.

Many men and women are busy finding their own gender identity. The women's movement and well-publicized behavioral models have neutralized the old tension between men and women in favor of brother-sister relationships. Many people are in search of models in which the masculine and feminine can be integrated into a new form such as the 'warrior of the heart' or the 'intelligent beauty'. Confronted by uncertainty about one's own masculine or feminine identity, many feel overstrained by the simultaneous demand to explore the unknown 'Other'. Communication becomes distorted by misunderstandings which result from the projection of one's own experiences, styles and behaviors onto the other gender.

Those couples who consciously choose the adventure of a relationship as a tool for growth can experiment with an astonishing spectrum of possible solutions, each demanding initiative, creativity and tolerance.

It is inherent in our open society that you can meet many people to whom you feel attracted, or whom you can imagine being with. If you cut off this impulse, you limit yourself in your own growth. People who attract you often open up areas that you cannot access with your partner. Such encounters are a sign that something is ripening in you that you would like to express.

Indeed, the question is how do you deal with such attractions. The answer depends on how you have managed the first two stages of development. Your progress in the earlier stages will determine how willing and able you are to commit yourself, and which values and principles are important in your life.

For many couples, infidelity is the critical issue which puts the relationship at risk. To avoid this risk, out of fear or for the sake of comfort, they restrict the complexity of their interests and modes of expression to the lowest common denominator. In the long run the relationship will be undermined thereby.

Unfaithfulness can mean different things in different cases. It can be an expression of an inability to commit to one partner on a deeper level. In this case the infidelity prevents a deeper commitment from emerging. It can also be a declaration of independence in a relationship where one partner, out of fear or personal insecurity, tries to control the other. In that case, the infidelity can break up rigid habits and structures and bring forth a new flow of energy.

On a more mature level, the impulse to break out of a relationship signals the need for expansion and exchange. If you confine this impulse to a network of friends, the expansion can bring enrichment to both partners.

The infringement of the sexual boundary is generally a threat which requires much tact and trust on both sides. There is no ready-made solution. A relationship has, like each person, its own stages of development. Each transition from one stage to the next carries deep changes. If you perceive these passages as crises, you may react with the fear of losing your partner.

The built-in response to the fear of loss is to cling to the partner or the past. If you understand the meaning of phrases such as 'opportunities for common growth', you are more capable of letting go and giving your partner space. Both of you can then reflect upon the common ground of the relationship and what new phase is about to birth.

How well you cope with such transitions will depend on your grounding in life, on the satisfaction you draw from your own realm of activity, and the circle of friends who are your resource. The ability to grow together requires that both partners be willing to unfold their personal potential.

Personal developments have their own rhythm, and often the rhythm of two partners does not coincide. This means that one partner may develop more quickly than the other. For the partner falling behind, this can be an incentive and a chance to expand their own field of vision and to realize more of their own potential. In some cases it may mean that you have to give your partner space so that they can find their own way. This works best if you focus on the fulfillment of your own life, independent of the partner. If you find that very difficult, it may be wise to seek help from a professional, or from couples who have mastered similar growth transitions.

How far your ways can move apart without risking the relationship depends on how much you value yourself, the commitment and openness of the relationship and your common experience in dealing with phases of growth. Here again, there is no ready-made solution. The more you trust yourself and your own way, the easier you can trust that your partner will find their way.

In some cases this may mean that your common task has come to an end and your ways separate. However instead of sinking into despair and loneliness, you will come out with a feeling of enrichment and gratitude for the gift that you have each been for the other.

### THE YES TO COMMUNITY

At this stage, if we feel close to another person, we also feel the need to share this closeness with others. Instead of gazing into each others' eyes, which would be the desire of the needy self, the eyes of both partners focus on a larger purpose which usually includes other people.

Humans are gregarious beings. Only in cooperation with others can they ensure the survival of the species. Traditionally, the family was the germ-cell of communities at all levels, from the neighborhood through organizations to the state.

With the decay of the traditional family as an economic unit, people have become more and more isolated and alone. In the last three decades the 'Human Potential' Movement has emerged as a counterforce. People gathered together in encounter groups and large group sessions to break through their shell of isolation. The anonymity of the encounter and the lack of commitment within those groups helped many participants to open their hearts and share their deeper feelings. Their next challenge was how to integrate these experiences into the routine of everyday life.

This was easier said than done, considering the pressure to perform and to compete in our Western culture. So people came together to create intentional communities with the aim of sharing their lives and developing new forms of living together. Such a community is the Findhorn Community in the northeast of Scotland in which I have lived and worked for the last 12 years.

It is no easy venture to explore new forms of communal living if there are no models to go by. The communities were, and still are, challenged by the same questions which confronted the whole sixties' generation which set out to change the world from a bureaucratic and rigid society to a humanized one.

What characterizes them as a generation is that they dispose of an excess of time and funds. This allows them to choose between, and to afford, a multitude of lifestyles. They are idealistic, dedicated and committed to ecologically healthy living conditions.

They have a high ideal of mankind, esteeming our species as a group of peers with equal rights, duties and desires. This manifests in demands for a radical-democratic social structure. In the ideal case, such a model means a 'free-flowing' hierarchy in which each person fulfills, according to his abilities, the next task in line. As needs change, people change their position accordingly.

The problem with such high aspirations is that it places heavy demands on all the people involved in the community: they should already have learned to care for their physical well-being and their environment; know their self worth; be able realistically to evaluate their strengths and weaknesses; and be capable of merging their personal interests with the common good.

The last point proves to be a critical one. People who are drawn to such communities gladly work in groups, and often they are very willing to sacrifice their own needs for their friends or the community. However, often this seeming strength is based on a weakness which originates in the needy self. This weakness is the fear of being excluded from the circle of friends. People are unwilling to put at risk the membership which was the reason for their joining the community in the first place.

This means that they are not ready to act alone or against the predominant opinion, even if their situation requires it. The abnegation of one's own interests in favor of the common good is thus accompanied by feelings of resentment, envy or inner protest. This may manifest in subliminal power struggles, self devaluation, or the devaluation of others. Such feelings can collectively solidify to a subliminal and mostly unconscious attitude which rejects all initiatives of the managing group, and in extreme cases this can paralyze the working of the community.

In the attempt to break open such structures, the community is confronted by its next challenge which I have already addressed in the section about addiction to suffering. This is the emergence of a subculture in which one's wounds become the content and the glue of communication.

To 'work' on one's own wounds satisfies the passion for personal growth while at the same time preventing a fundamental and lasting personality change which would include the assumption of personal responsibility and accountability. To assume responsibility risks exclusion from the community, especially in face of the collective resistance to change.

An apparent solution combines both the need for personal growth and the fear of assuming responsibility. This is 'to be in process'. 'To be in process' means to 'work' on one's wounds. Working on one's wounds can become an aim in itself. It creates a safe structure, while at the same time it justifies one's not pursuing any other outside goals.

The subculture supports this withdrawal from responsibility in two ways. On the one hand, 'being in process' justifies one's withdrawal from obligations in common projects without risking the affection of others. On the other hand, the community offers justifying strategies which allow one to seek for the enemy outside, instead of looking inside at one's own driving forces and one's weaknesses in respect to them.

However, if in the process of passing through the stages of development the needy self has matured, other possibilities open up for dealing with communities or systems on the different levels.

The matured self has overcome its fears of survival and is therefore free to work on its own or with others, depending on need. This does not mean that it does not get depressed. It notices and acknowledges such feelings, but it does not let them influence its decisions. Feelings come and go. More essential is attitude and behavior. For the matured self, failure is not misfortune but information and a learning experience.

The matured self is not afraid of power nor is it attracted by it. It knows how to get it and how to use it, but it also knows how limited is its usefulness.

The matured self can postpone personal interests in favor of the common good. It does this, not out of fear, but out of the knowledge that we are all linked with each other. It knows that its actions ultimately reflect back on itself.

The matured self feels committed to the preservation of life and this world. It aims to produce abundance which serves everybody.

### THE YES TO HUMAN VALUES

The matured self which has satisfactorily passed through the stages of development and made friends with its shadow side, naturally and organically adopts the universal principles that link mankind, independent of culture and race. Among them are love, trust, truth, peace, non-violence, justice, honesty and wisdom.

All the great teachers of mankind have recommended these qualities as desirable goals and guidelines for life. And yet it is a long road to 'become' these qualities, to live them as a natural result of one's own development. It requires that you come to terms with your 'demons', your shadow side, the negative emotions of anger, envy, jealousy, fear, grief and worries, and that you learn to lovingly embrace those emotions.

Through your acceptance and embrace, they change into the positive qualities which are their reverse sides. If you neglect this work, you risk deceiving yourself. The perfect or grandiose self, which I have addressed in the section about 'the YES to the self', likes to pretend that it already owns these positive qualities. Since it must be perfect, it can not allow the shadow side to exist. It suppresses the negative qualities so that they are not accessible to your conscious mind anymore.

You may have an image of yourself which is not shared by your acquaintances, colleagues or friends. They may make you painfully aware of the discrepancy between your aspirations and your reality. To be made conscious of such a discrepancy is burdensome to the grandiose self, and it reacts with feelings of failure, guilt and shame.

If you reflect on what the realization of human values really means when lived in life, the understanding can be a great relief for your unfolding self.

"To love your neighbor as yourself' requires that you can love yourself.

Honesty requires that you can see through family programs and cultural guidelines.

Non-violence presupposes that you have come to terms with your own inner conflicts and have made peace between your different impulses and quirks.

Trust requires that you can rely on yourself and see others as they are, so that you do not trust blindly and end up in disappointment.

Wisdom comes from experience and the knowledge of human fragility and insufficiency. This knowledge makes us humble and keeps the grandiose self in bounds.

As you can see, living those principles is a path for the elucidation of your learning purpose and your strengths and weaknesses. It is not something which you can expect to acquire by right. It is something into which we mature bit by bit. Give yourself the time and space for its accomplishment, and avoid making too heavy demands on yourself which will only cause you to miscarry.

### THE YES TO THE UNION WITH LIFE

On the universal level, the grandiose self likes to present itself as the true, divine self, your core which is at one with the universe and the cosmos.

Its 'masks' on this level are manifold. It is easy to get fooled. Be aware of the trap it sets for you if you have not yet mastered your physical existence. The self tends to be grandiose if it is not rooted in life, that is in physical existence. It may think that it knows the absolute truth, which it then imposes on others without regard to their situation and state of development.

The real 'divine' self, our inner core, is aware of the relativity of truth. It knows that we are all on our path and that each one of us must recognize the truth for ourselves. The 'divine' self pays attention to where others stand in their life and respects their right 'to be' in that place. Others do not have to change in order to satisfy its world view. It supports others in being and doing what is right for them, and leaves to them the decision how fast they want to change, and even whether they want to change at all.

As compared to the grandiose self, the 'divine' self completes the cycle and brings us back to our physical existence. It knows that it has to manifest itself within the physical world before it can start its journey home. It also knows that we are part of a larger whole, so it takes care not to get entangled in the pitfalls of this world. It is in this world, without being of this world.

# The Spiral Staircase

## OUR LIFE PATTERNS AS SIGNPOSTS

As a child, I learned that life extends from birth to death through a vale of tears, a one-time happening so to speak, which according to God's will would end with heaven or hell. Which fate one met would be no whimsical accident. Obedience rather than originality provided the better chance of heaven. Naturally, I did my very best to qualify for heaven.

This was no simple venture, considering the inconsistent statements and demands directed at me from different sides. To complicate matters further, my innermost nature did not bow easily to those demands. So I drew the logical conclusion and decided to get rid of this rebellious part that was doing its best to muff my chances of heaven. I went into psychoanalysis.

There came the session when I was complaining of how sick I obviously was, as I had done on many previous occasions. I had not succeeded in fulfilling my mother's ideal, which was to strive for a happy life as a housewife and mother in a suburban terrace house. After a long pause, I heard my psychoanalytical mother say, "It seems to me that you confuse something here. Your rebellious part is your healthy part, and your efforts to adjust to outer demands is the sick one."

I thought I had not heard aright. Were all the years that I had struggled against this untamed urge for freedom for nothing? Should precisely that part be healthy that saw in others the things they did not know about themselves, or did not want to know? That part be healthy which, if I merely opened my mouth, infuriated the people in my neighborhood? My view of life was dealt a heavy blow. And quite a few years were to pass until I recognized that life was not the way it had been told me in my childhood.

Instead of a journey leading straight from birth to death, my life unfolded like a spiral staircase. On the way into deeper and deeper layers of my being, I passed by the same patterns. However, I perceived them from different angles, until their content had completely revealed itself and I could leave them behind.

I found my process described in Portia Nelson's *Autobiography in Five Short Chapters.*

| | |
|---|---|
| *Chapter One* | *I walk down the street.* |
| | *There is a deep hole in the sidewalk.* |
| | *I fall in.* |
| | *I am lost,* |
| | *I am helpless,* |
| | *It isn't my fault.* |
| | *It takes me forever to find a way out.* |
| *Chapter Two* | *I walk down the same street.* |
| | *There is a deep hole in the sidewalk.* |
| | *I pretend I do not see it.* |
| | *I fall in again.* |
| | *I cannot believe I am in the same place.* |
| | *But it isn't my fault.* |
| | *It still takes a long time to get out.* |

| Chapter Three | *I walk down the same street.* |
| --- | --- |
| | *There is a deep hole in the sidewalk.* |
| | *I see it is there.* |
| | *I still fall in;* |
| | *It is a habit.* |
| | *But my eyes are open,* |
| | *I know where I am.* |
| | *It is my fault.* |
| | *I get out immediately.* |
| Chapter Four | *I walk down the same street.* |
| | *There is a deep hole in the sidewalk.* |
| | *I walk around it.* |
| Chapter Five | *I walk down another street.* |

If you pay attention to repetitive patterns in your life, you will probably notice that a particular theme keeps coming back and that it extends from small to big events. For example, if your challenge is to feel betrayed or taken advantage of by others, you may encounter such situations when you go to the bakery to pick up rolls, and also in your personal relationships and in financial agreements with business partners.

In the course of life you throw light on such a pattern from different angles. In that way you explore it until it has fulfilled its function and you can let it go. At that moment you walk down another street.

## THE CYCLE OF MANIFESTATION

### THE FIVE ELEMENTS

In the section about the Holographic Universe I described how pulsating patterns of energy waves cross each other's circles and form what is called an interference pattern.[25] According to our understanding of reality as a hologram, there is a subtler realm of relationships and energy flows that underlie the unfolded order which is our visible world. This subtle realm, or enfolded order, embraces the interference patterns and is not visible to our eyes, but determines our thoughts, feelings and physical processes.

---

[25] Compare 'The Reality As Hologram' and 'Unfolded And Enfolded Realities' in the Section: The Holographic Universe

The Ayurvedic tradition of India, and also Chinese medicine, describe the motive forces which weave themselves into interference patterns as five elements. To these they assign specific qualities of energy and consciousness. These elements are called ether, air, fire, water and earth. They flow out of five energy centers in our body which are called chakras and which are each related to one of the elements.[26]

Chakras are vortex-like energy centers which pick up and distribute impulses within the energy system of the body. Traditionally, we speak of seven chakras, each associated with different body zones. The two highest chakras, which are the crown chakra on the highest point of the head and the third eye in the forehead, reach beyond the five elements. Of those associated with the elements, the chakra center of ether is located at the throat, that of air at the heart, fire at the navel center, water in the pelvic area, and earth in the anal region at the junction of the sacrum and coccyx.

Each element represents a quality of energy and consciousness, and these flow out of the associated chakra. The higher in the body that the chakra is located, the subtler is the energy and the more expansive the level ofconsciousness. As the energy gets stepped down through the chakras, it gets coarser and the consciousness is more restricted. For example, the quality of universal love is the quality of the element air in the heart chakra. If the love impulse arises out of the water element in the pelvic area, it becomes sexual desire.

You can liken the chakras to transformers which at each downward step transform the energy into a denser form until finally at the earth element it becomes crystallized into the physical forms which we can perceive with our senses.

This process is called manifestation, or the conversion of energy into form. You can observe this process in nature, as when water turns to ice or conversely, into steam. Great teachers of mankind such as Sai Baba have dominion over the laws of this cycle, which they demonstrate when they manifest material objects seemingly out of air.

I said before that chakras are vortex-like energy centers. A vortex is a basic energy form in the universe. For instance, they manifest as swirls in a river or as hurricanes in the air. It is due to the importance of the vortex as a fundamental element of the universe that our life does not proceed linearly

---

[26] I owe the inspiration to this section to Chloe Wordsworth's *Life Cycle Repatterning*. Compare also the excellent book by Franklyn Sills: The Polarity Process. Shaftesbury: Element Books 1989

but cyclically, like a spiral with up- or downward trend. A spiral is the combination of a circle and an arrow. The circle includes the spectrum of our experiences on one level while the arrow points to the direction, up or down. If we apply this spiral movement to our daily life, we can recognize our life's path as a spiral staircase. According to the holographic law that each part contains the whole, we find this spiral process happening alike in small and large areas of our life.

In the last section we looked at the different stages of development through which we pass in a continuous expansion of consciousness. You can visualize this process as an upward winding spiral staircase. On each level of the staircase, we run through a cycle of five steps in order to manifest a thought form. As we move upwards, it is necessary to complete one level before going on to the next. Inversely, this is the same process as that taken by a thought from its first impulse to its materialized form; or the process through which the divine self passes in order to concretize itself in matter.

This process has its challenges and pitfalls. Depending on how you perceive and process life, as described in the section on 'Finding the True Self', you may feel more drawn to one style than to the others. In the following pages, I will describe the specific qualities of the five elements and their related pitfalls.

## ETHER

We begin with Ether, the void, the formless and creative space from which all impulses originate. This is the space of stillness which you reach in deep meditation. It corresponds to the larynx-chakra.

The stillness which is Ether allows you to enter the primordial ground of the universal mind. The individual consciousness is a part of it. When you are at one with this primordial ground, the creative potential of the universe is available to create the things in your life that are in harmony with this all-inclusive mind. In this process you become a channel through which the creative mind expresses itself in order to serve others. The condition is that you immerse yourself in the stillness and there stand fast. Your intuitive perception will sense which mode is your individual expression of this universal mind. The goal is to realize your uniqueness, and your unique contribution to life.

The primordial ground is the space of unlimited potential. With my inner eye I see it like a black untouched plain from which small promontories break forth like air bubbles and sink back again. These promontories are the

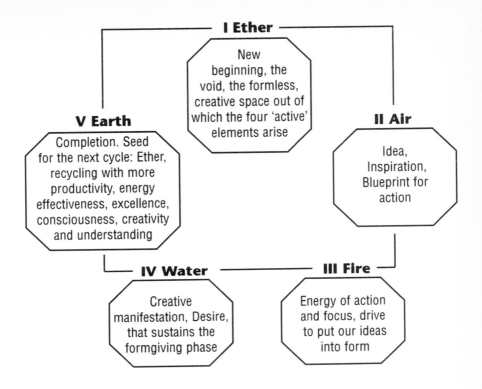

**Figure 3: The Cycle of Manifestation**

thoughts and ideas which set things in motion so that they manifest themselves in matter. Sometimes an idea breaks forth like a flash from the unlimited potential of the primordial ground, sometimes it takes longer to track the thought impulse down.

The Ether center positioned in the neck is a place where the thoughts, emotions and sensations of mind and body interconnect. In its physical capacity as an organ of expression, the larynx is a center of communication between our inside areas and the outside world. Through this center you express your higher truth and your creative spirit, as well as your everyday needs, feelings and opinions.

Ether is the neutral, passive space out of which the other four elements unfold. Each of these elements, air, fire, water and earth represents a quality of movement which expresses itself in bodily processes. The manner in which these elements combine creates the manner in which we bring our ideas and feelings into the world.

## AIR

The element Air governs movement in general. Air can be like the brisk breeze that refreshes us on a hot summer day or it can blast us like a tempest.

Thinking belongs to the Air element; those thoughts which as mental movement take shape as ideas, concepts or plans which we strive to realize in our lives.

If the element of Air is in balance, we are open to new ideas and approaches. If the flow is congested or stagnant, we may instead hold onto our concepts and thoughts and refuse to budge. If the Air element is dominant, we may enjoy playing with concepts and ideas but find it difficult to get in touch with our feelings and bodily sensations. We may also find it a struggle to ground or complete our projects.

Each thought is a vibratory field that, according to the law of attraction, draws in the necessary information, tools, circumstances, people and finances. For a thought to become reality, it must be clear, precise and constant. A thought which is only an aggregation of constantly changing thought impulses does not have enough power to crystallize as form. Strong, ambivalent ideas appear in realized form as a sequence of inconsistent or confusing situations, which are actually attempts to express the diversity of the different thought impulses.

The most successful way to give a thought a clear and precise form is by a mental image which we impress on our right brain, and thus on our subconscious. This process is called visualization. In this process we identify in our inner world with the object or the condition which we wish to bring into physical reality. We become this thing or condition, and this thing or condition becomes part of us. The be-ingness, the unity of I and It, provides it with the necessary strength to endure the long journey through the matrix of creation from the idea to the form.

Air is connected to the heart center. In popular usage, the heart is the seat of the soul and of love. Because the heart chakra lies closest to Ether which is the primordial ground of being, the love of the heart has the all-embracing quality which is not bound up with ego needs. It is indeed the pure and conscious desire that longs to return to its source. The thought-impulses which are nurtured from this source are connected to heart qualities such as love, joy, compassion, gratitude, abundance and service to others.

## FIRE

Air is the thought impulse, but to bring idea and concept into reality, you need the active energy of Fire. Fire is an expansive force which gives direction to the movement of Air. As it relates to mental processes, it creates a 'fiery intellect' or a 'quickness of mind'.

Fire gives one the ability to keep focused on the goal and carry on a project through all difficulties. Fire nourishes the thought impulse even in the face of great resistance and gathers the necessary energy for the impulse to take physical form. Fire, which is drive, focus and stamina, transforms any mere possibility into a conscious act of creation.

When your Fire element is balanced, you love life and move enthusiastically into action. You act without thinking overmuch. You have stamina and a clear mind capable of cutting through turmoil and confusion.

If you suppress your Fire, you may experience a seething resentment against the world or even self-denigration and a sense of depression and powerlessness. If the Fire element dominates your personality, you may become too self-centered and strong willed and try to force your will on others, if necessary with violence.

Fire is associated with the navel center and the Solar Plexus. The navel center is the seat of your vital energy which gives you focus and stamina. The Solar Plexus, or sun center, distributes warmth throughout the body and radiates it out as light into the world. It is this light which draws in the resources to assist you in realizing your purpose.

Fire is connected with the negative emotions of anger and resentment. However, if you use their potential in a positive way, you gain self-assertion and intellectual clarity of mind from their reversal.

## WATER

Water supports the drive, focus and stamina of the Fire element. Water is the energy of deep feelings and desire which draws the thought impulse through the creation matrix into physical reality.

In contrast to the rational pole of the Air element, Water is the irrational pole of feelings which drive our actions out of the depths of the Unconscious. This sort of knowledge is not determined by the rational mind but by intuitive understanding of the laws of the universe and their relationships, and of how the world is interpreted emotionally.

Compared to the expansive quality of the Air element, Water is a contractive force. It grounds the energy of Air, bringing thoughts or concepts to Earth. Water seeks its lowest level. It anchors the ideas deep into the ground and gives them shape.

Water also has a receptive quality. It accepts all things. It is the feminine and nurturing part in us which brings healing and growth to all our levels.

Water is the element of the sacral chakra, between the fifth lumbar vertebra and the sacrum. It is linked to the pelvic area with all its sexual impulses, but also has the ability to eliminate whatever does not serve the system. The misuse of power, be it of a sexual, financial or emotional nature, has its roots in this area, as have the related fears of powerlessness and subjugation, and of sexual guilt and shame.

If the Water element flows freely, you get in touch with your feelings in a very grounded way. You are able to process and work through emotional patterns much in the way that water flows around stones and in time polishes them to roundness. If the flow of Water is blocked, you will have the tendency to hold on to things or people. This relates especially to sexual desires and needs. Or you may drown in feelings of grief, depression and despair, unfulfilled longing and lusts.

If the Water element is in balance with the Air element, you will have a fluid and flexible mind. You are open to new insights and capable of changing the direction of your decisions if circumstances require. The combination of idea and desire generates the power to draw forth whatever is necessary to allow the seed of thought to grow and ripen. For us, the challenge of this form-giving Water phase is that we do not block the flow by initiating our own plan of action. The universal mind knows much better than we, with our limited experience, what ways best serve our goal.

## EARTH

The last stage in the cycle of manifestation is Earth. Earth is the realm of experience where you interact with this world through your senses, and where your thoughts and actions finally crystallize. Earth is where you harvest the fruits of your work.

Earth has mass and therefore inertia. In your daily life you may find yourself struggling with the resistance inherent in mass. For example, you may resist getting up in the morning, doing your exercises or overcoming your negative habits. Your physical form, that is your body, can feel like a prison to your mind and soul. On the other hand, Earth gives you the steadiness and perseverance to follow through on all the many practical steps and little details that are necessary to complete a project.

If the Earth element is dominant, you may find yourself stuck in daily routines, or feel limited in imagination and intuition when new ideas or experiences present themselves. If the element is weak, you may find it difficult to complete your projects. You can easily become lost in your daydreams or drowned in feelings.

Earth is one step down from Water and its energy is even more contractive. On the emotional level, this may express itself in a withdrawal and constriction of your energy which you then experience as fear. Fear on this level relates to issues of physical safety and survival. You may be afraid that your survival needs are not being met, or feel that you don't belong, or that you have no home or no support.

Earth is the element of the root-chakra situated between the sacrum and coccyx. It is the root of the backbone which serves us as foundation, support and grounding. If your backbone is weak or bent, it will be mirrored in the different areas of your life. If somebody is afraid to take action, we say, "He has no backbone."

In the cycle of manifestation, the Earth element is the utmost point of contraction, where the energy flow has lost its impetus and crystallized into form. Potentially, it is the point of return to our source and the springboard for the next cycle. To use its potential aright, we need to be fully in the here and now and harvest the fruits of our work without clinging to the past or dreaming of the future.

## PITFALLS

Each of these steps in the cycle of manifestation has its pitfalls.

### ETHER

During the first phase of the process, within the stillness which is the Ether chakra, it is important that you become conscious of your unity with the universal mind. Only then can you gain access to the creative potential.

The first pitfall is that the individual consciousness usually acts like a pond which is cut off from the ocean. Unless you dig your way back to your original source, you have little chance of starting the creative process.

The second pitfall is one set by the Christian church. Christians understand the process of manifestation as the outcome of a type of prayer where God is an outer authority to whom you come as a petitioner. God can grant your request or refuse it. If your request is granted, the things or events you desire are conveyed to you. There is a dual quality to the relationship between yourself and God, for he may act either as a punishing or supportive parent. But no matter how he acts, God sits on his throne above you, and in this dual relationship you are asking from a position of lack. According to the law of resonance, lack can only generate lack. In the dual relationship, people often attach to the divine the traits of parents or other important authority figures. Since these relationships are marked by human insufficiencies, they get translated into one's relationship with God and create doubts, tension and stress. These negative feelings hinder, weaken or prevent the creative act.

However, if you are conscious of your oneness with the universal mind, you work in creative partnership with the divine. You become the channel through which the divine can express itself. You find this knowledge in the New Testament where Jesus tells a hostile crowd that the Son can do nothing of himself, but what he sees the Father do, the Son does likewise.

Ether has its location in the throat and neck area which connects body and mind. This is an area which for many people in our culture is blocked, congested or cut off. You may experience this as a feeling of fear or an incapacity to speak your truth and ask for what you want. To compensate, you may use your willpower to impose yourself on others, manipulating them or even using force to gratify your needs.

Your resistance to expressing your needs and desires may prevent you from even perceiving them. The truth can be so deeply veiled that you may not notice that you are deceiving yourself.

If you cut off the connection between your body and your mind, it will be hard to endure the silence and get in touch with your deeper needs. You may have experienced occasions when you allowed your tears to flow and your mind suddenly opened up to new insights and ideas that would never have come to you otherwise, no matter how hard you strained your brain. Your inner guide[27] may give you the protection and confidence necessary to risk the silence and become aware of that in you which would like to connect and express itself.

---

[27] Compare 'The Journey To The Inner Self' in the section about Self-Realization and 'The Inner Guide' in the section about Transformation

## Air

When, in the silence, thoughts and ideas take shape, beware that you are not just daydreaming or building beautiful castles in the air. Be honest about your capabilities and skills, your motives and the options available to you. Honesty will include an understanding of the time that certain procedures may take. Some goals are life-long tasks that you approach step by step over a long period. Learn to discipline your thoughts to the point that you consciously select them, and sculpt what you have selected.

Initially, this is a learning process. Many people can say what they do not want, but find it very difficult to say what they do. There are many reasons for this. One that I have just mentioned is the separation between mind and body. Other reasons have to do with our cultural and social conditioning.

In some circles it is considered improper to have needs, or even to express them. Many people know basically what they want, but think they do not have the right to make demands or that they risk the love of others by doing so. Therefore they do not even begin to formulate their wants. It saves them the frustration of not getting them. Or else they are not able to formulate their wants because they have not learned to think precisely and clearly. The jargon of the last two decades does not encourage a differentiated use of

language. Other people avoid committing themselves. They do not want to commit themselves even to their own goals. They prefer to keep them vague so that there is always a loophole through which they can escape the consequences.

Another pitfall has to do with a person's contradictory motives. He may want things which are mutually exclusive or can only be reconciled on the next higher level. Many people, for example, wish for a partner who is there for them without being equally ready to be there for the partner. Or they would like to have a lot of money without being ready to do something to get it. These contradictions originate from immature, infantile needs which a person must first mature and then bring into harmony with each other in order to draw forth one's desire from the universal mind.

Some people believe that they have no talent for inner images or visualizations. Their mind is afraid that it will lose control if they engage with their inner world. Or else they have a predetermined idea of what an inner image or visualization should look like, so that they do not recognize the inner images when they do emerge. This problem can easily be solved with some experience and good instruction.

### FIRE

Fire is an energy which can overwhelm and destroy us if we do not know how to contain and direct it. We usually think of people being afraid of death, but more often they fear the vitality of life and its untamed nature if they should lose control.

This fear can be absolutely legitimate. In my sessions with clients, Fire frequently emerges as a menace in sexual intimacy, causing thunder, lightning and general chaos in all areas of life, and ultimately burning the instigator. Or the Fire may unfold its uncontrollable power in the Solar Plexus, and rising into the head break out in anger, power games or undirected aggression.

In the traditional cultures there were Fire Guards, often wise women, who knew how to use the qualities of the Fire in such a way that everybody in the tribe could best profit from it. They had the ability to preserve it, keep the people warm at its flames, nourish them and protect them from attacks of wild animals.

In our culture we have largely lost the ability to handle this life energy appropriately. We burn out. We are lacking a solid, well built oven to keep the Fire in place and at the same time use its power to maintain a constant heat. There are many people who feel themselves driven restlessly hither and thither and waste their energy in senseless acts. Others keep their energy on a low flame so as not to provoke any change or discomfort. In consequence, the Fire does not have the power to draw into their lives the things which they desire.

We should learn to bring the sexual Fire under the control of the heart so that this energy can be used for love and joy. Let your light shine and draw into your life those things, people and events which you need. Contained and directed Fire gives you perseverance and continuity, two qualities that are worth cultivating if you want to grow through joy.

### WATER

Dealing with the flow of life has its hurdles. Water finds its own way. It is the soft power which breaks the stone and sneaks through, taking everything with it. Water is also the receptacle of our power, our reservoir from which we draw if we keep it well filled.

Water stands for the feelings, desires or wishes. You can use the power of desire and conduct the flow in your chosen direction, or you can allow your wishes to control you. Then you are subject to moods which drive you now here, now there. These mood swings prevent your ideas from taking shape. You remain attached to a dreamlike world which is filled with unconscious responses to childhood experiences.

If you attach yourself to the fulfillment of your desires, you become dependent on them and you will do anything to satisfy them. With that, you divert your energy from the fulfillment of your ideas towards the lower frequencies of your moody needs and wishes. When you are so attached, you are at the same time blocking the ways in which the universal mind would like to support you in fulfillment of your plans.

Fears and doubts are the other water aspects by which you prevent your ideas from taking shape. Fears and doubts reverse the flow of manifestation to the opposite direction, away from you. Fears and doubts cause you to repel the things which you would like to have, so that they cannot come together to manifest the idea or concept. Fear is the negative pole of attraction, the arch-enemy of love. Fear is the law of repulsion.

### EARTH

Earth is completion and at the same time it is the seed for the next cycle. Many people are not aware of the importance of this last step. They are in the habit of leaving unfinished business which takes up a large part of their energy and snares them in a repetitive noose. Instead of moving forward to the next level, they run around in circles. Unfinished business is relevant to all areas of life. It is the overfilled dustbin in your apartment which reminds you, each time you pass by, that you are a slut; it is the ragged piece of material on the chair which tells of your inability to attend to things promptly; it is the stack of unfinished work on top of the TV which means that you cannot enjoy your free time.

The pile of unfinished business reminds me of 'rechauds', those little containers with a candle inside that Europeans use to keep their tea or coffee warm. Many people have set up a whole system of such rechauds to avoid their being alone. Instead of committing themselves to one person or task, they keep many on a low flame so that they can always fall back on somebody or something if necessary.

Unfinished business ensures that your energy is scattered. When you allow this to happen, you guarantee that you will not begin anything new, because you have not completed the old.

In its negative form, Earth is one's need for safety which results from the pond situation. If you do not believe that there is an ocean which provides you with new water, you will defend your pond against all comers. You use your energy to satisfy your own needs without taking the needs of others into account. From the perspective of the pond, other people are a potential threat and not companions. You hold on to what you have and prevent any change from happening. With that, you seal off the open paradigm of the spiral staircase and withdraw into a closed system.

## A CASE EXAMPLE

The process of building my house at Findhorn illustrates how the elements operate in the cycle of manifestation, both their correct application and the pitfalls which attend them.

The seed of the idea was set in the **Ether**. Years before I had heard of Findhorn, with my inner eye I saw for a split second a wooden house standing in a circle of other wooden houses which I had built in an English speaking community. When, much later, I came to Findhorn for the first time, I recognized the place.

From Ether, the thought impulse descends to the domain of **Air** for its concrete modeling. In my case, this part of the creative process took quite a bit of time. In that snapshot of my future, I saw that I had built a wooden house. However, a wooden house can take many different forms when it comes to detailed planning. It took several years of intense research to give this impulse a concept: an ecological house with breathing walls and a balanced combination of space, light and warmth.

**Fire** provides the impetus to drive the thought impulse through all difficulties. That spontaneous vision of my house proved to be a decisive element in ensuring its implementation. My savings had not anticipated such a project. So I could only trust that the laws of manifestation that had been tested in Findhorn would also work in my case. I just had to learn to apply them correctly.

The element of **Water** gives form to a thought. Many steps are necessary on the physical plane. The art is to be attentive to whatever unexpected help comes along, while at the same time taking the necessary steps to manifest the intent. This requires that one be willing to endure uncomfortable situations while remaining open to new possibilities. The form-giving process is a subtle balance between one's own activity and allowing things to unfold.

Uncomfortable situations soon materialized. Through endless discussions, I began to find a third way between community interests and private initiative. This challenge touched all areas: planning, finances, the legal framework and the construction work itself. I explored models of ecological buildings and together with an architect, compiled plans for the building of the house. I chose my construction crew and found myself confronted with a number of building decisions to be made on site when my architect followed his inner voice to the Himalayas at the beginning of the actual building process. After a good five months, I had spent my last possible pennies and in short order found myself compelled to master the necessary skills to complete the interior works.

First, I focused my willpower to complete the project at the set deadline, but in so doing, I interposed myself between the project and the universal mind. After a long phase of inner doubts, I came to understand that I could not finish it just by my willpower alone. I surrendered to my fate and allowed the universal mind to hurry up and help me. And to my surprise, the unexpected happened. People from the Findhorn Foundation came and helped with the time-consuming work of painting the wood and the walls. Friends offered furniture so that I could equip the house as a B&B, and the international currency market, which had swallowed my only investment, shifted its parameters in such a way that the missing money for financing the house was suddenly available.

**Earth** signifies completion and renewal. At the deadline, my 45th birthday, I opened up the house as a B&B. It would still be another year before I recovered from my physical exhaustion. During that time I equipped the interior with curtains, bed covers and my own furniture, and outside I laid the seeds for a beautiful garden. The new cycle would be to spend time in the house with my guests and friends.

# The Choice Point: Drama Or Joy

If you had the choice between joy or drama in your life, which would you choose? You would probably say joy. But think about it. Would you really be willing to give up your drama for the sake of joy? Or do you think that joy and drama can exist side by side?

They cannot. Drama and joy exclude each other. Drama is fed by feelings of self devaluation, suffering and failure. It confirms one's notion of worthlessness and legitimates one's suffering. Drama is like a downward spiral which takes us ever further into the swamp. The further and deeper it grinds down, the more it has the character of a self-destructive addiction.

For many people their life drama is the basis of their identity. Their aim in life is to gain recognition of the suffering they have endured. This is a very human and legitimate need. The problem with drama is that recognizing the suffering does not cure it. On the contrary. The knowledge that it gets you attention and compassion from others gives the drama additional value. It becomes a tool for gaining affection. The drama is thereby strengthened, and it becomes even more difficult to free yourself from its grip.

For many people, their daily small catastrophes are also a way to feel alive. Sometimes, it is the only way they know how to feel alive. Drama is fed by the intensity and high voltage of one's feelings. Our present time is still permeated by the notion current in the sixties and seventies, that catharsis of the feelings means to be alive.

You may have participated in weekend seminars and encounter groups where you saw people get up on stage and expose their innermost feelings. For many years I have watched the process with shock and fascination, and once I even tried it myself. I watched with fascination because it is something I find hard to do, and with shock because the performances looked so rehearsed that I wondered whether such an approach could really solve the suffering.

I also participated in other groups where people came in touch with their inner pain or deep-rooted patterns in a silent way. As they became conscious of them, those patterns lost their power. The difference between the two procedures is the high voltage and intensity connected with gaining the insight on the one hand and the quiet approach on the other.

The real changes mostly come in small and inconspicuous steps, and often you only notice them when you look back and realize that you are no longer reacting as you once did. Instead of jumping up when your colleague makes a pointed remark, you suddenly notice that she is not well and that her comment has nothing to do with you. Instead of sinking into self-doubt and shame when somebody criticizes you for a particular behavior, you suddenly feel at ease. You may even feel grateful that somebody has pointed out your lack of awareness.

I often see people in my practice who cannot even imagine how it feels to be alive without running on high voltage. The joy that emerges from the stillness and fills the inner being appears boring by comparison, especially if that experience is not at first accessible and must be developed through daily practice. One must have faith that this daily practice will guide one out of the swampland, especially when success is not immediately noticeable.

Your best chance of success comes when you arrive at that point in life when you are tired of the drama, and the drawbacks of suffering have become stronger than the goodies which you get from it. I call this the choice point. The pull of the drama and your self-destructive part is balanced by your desire to live a fulfilling and rewarding life. If you can say one hundred percent yes to life, the scales will come down in your favor. Then you switch from a downward to an upward spiral. Your work is not yet finished, but it becomes a lot easier because satisfactory experiences now accelerate the upward movement.

The question is, how do you get to this choice point.

There is a broad spectrum of techniques and methods which aim at dissolving old structures and establishing new ways of thinking and acting. The transformation of drama into joy is a reciprocal process. Step by step you cultivate the joy so that the drama energy has a container into which it can flow and transform. The stronger the container of joy becomes, the more you dissolve the dynamic of suffering, and the more you dissolve that, the stronger you can make the container of joy.

I meet many people who are so attached to their drama that they cannot think how to extricate themselves. If such is the case, you may need a therapist to help you become conscious of your identification with suffering and the causative factors in your past experience. You then can build up the necessary trust and the daily discipline which will lead you to the choice point.

You may need to shop around to find out which of the many tools within the therapeutic and spiritual realm appeal to you. There is a broad market of possibilities. What attracts you naturally as a daily practice has the best chance for success.

Whatever path you follow, there are some basic principles which have proven valuable across times and cultures. They are simple and powerful, so simple indeed that we find it hard to believe that they work.

The first consideration is that many people lack the necessary inner and physical strength to do what is good for them, in spite of all their knowledge and good intentions. Their own self-destructive part wins again and again over their best intent. In such cases, the first step is to build up the inner and physical strength.

Many people have formed no inner picture of how their life could be different. They are lacking in imagination, models and goals. They do not know who they are, what they are doing and what they would like to have. If the reason is lack of practice, it is easy to change that. A few good directions will help you form and develop your power of visualization.

In other cases, the inner stage is so occupied by threatening figures and monsters that there is no space left for positive configurations. Day dreams or fantasies dominate the inner realm instead of consciously created mental images. Usually, they correspond little to reality, but balance feelings of unworthiness, guilt and shame.

In such cases, you first need to create the necessary space by transforming those threatening figures and monsters into allies. The key is that you should understand what gift these monsters bring you. Usually they protect your life or dignity. If you free the monsters from their dark cave in the Unconscious and recognize their purpose, they lose their power to threaten. They take on a more mature form and become allies who help you get a grip on your life.

Good instructions may be all that is necessary for some people to transform these monsters. Others may first need therapeutic support before they acquire the necessary self-confidence to handle these inner figures.

The following section will give you detailed instructions on how to change deep-rooted patterns of suffering into life enhancing patterns of joy. It is a manual which uses my therapeutic and personal experience and case material to demonstrate techniques which you can apply in your daily life.

# The Basic Pulsation Of Life

## THE RHYTHM OF BREATH

Breath is the source of the power within, and of our physical strength. Breath is rhythm, rhythm is polarity, and polarity pervades all aspects of the human being. The basic function of inbreath and outbreath corresponds on the physical level to the muscle functions of expansion and contraction, on the emotional level to the polarity of love (expansion) and fear (contraction), and on the social level to the balance between being with oneself and being with others.

Even the cycles of life which I described in the last section follow the principles of polarity. As we are born and project ourselves out into the world, we expand and unfold our potential. When we reach middle age, the energy contracts and we harvest the fruits of our work through middle age, old age and death. Death is a return to our beginnings, a transition into the next cycle.

If we expand our awareness even further, we find that in the esoteric tradition the whole universe is an expression of God's in-breath and out-breath. As God breathes in, he expands the universe until it reaches its outer surface, which in its coarsest form is our physical world. This 'involutionary' movement is followed by his outbreath, a contraction or an 'evolutionary' phase in which we get pulled back to the source. Each breath of God completes one cosmic day that extends over billions of years.[28]

These two phases, inbreath and outbreath, expansion and contraction, involution and evolution, create the Basic Pulsation of Life. All aspects of life mirror this process. Just think of the change of the seasons, when during the

---

[28] According to Joshua D. Stone the length of a cosmic day equals 4.3 billion years. In accordance with the prophecies of the Mayan calender the exact moment between the inbreath and outbreath of God will occur in 2012. Compare: Joshua D. Stone: *The Complete Ascension Manual.* Sedona: Light Technology Publishing 1994. Section 1 and Section 20

winter months energy gets contracted back into its source. If you think of plants, the energy gets focused back into the bulbs and roots to strengthen them for the outburst in spring that expands the life force outwards into growth and splendor during the height of summer. In fall, the plants die back, and the energy gets pulled back to its source for a new cycle of contraction and expansion, or involution and evolution. If you look at the human body, it is the expansion and contraction of the lungs and the heart that keeps us alive by pumping oxygen through our blood. You can feel that pulse when you put your fingers on your wrist. The body is a pulsating field of energy, and if your energy is free to move you may experience this as a streaming force that pulses through your cells, systems and organs.

I well remember the overwhelming feeling when I first experienced this pulsating force streaming through my body. It had taken me a good ten years of daily Tao Yoga and meridian stretching exercises, body therapy and rolfing to realign and re-awaken my body to its own life force.

In our everyday language we call the movement of these two phases, rhythm. Our language expresses the meaning of rhythm in many ways.

If you are healthy and vital, you are in-tact. When you relate to other people, you have con-tact. If you are sensitive to the needs of others and you respect their dignity, you are tact-full. If you have trouble in discerning the distinction between yourself and others, you are in danger of being tact-less. And if when dancing, you step on your partner's toes, you have probably lost the beat or your sense of tact.

Rhythm is composed of a polar movement. We open ourselves up to the outside and take in universal energies. We then turn inside and collect, digest and integrate the intake. Both movements are equally important and need the same time and attention.

Rhythm is heart beat. Our first contact with it is in our mother's womb. In the course of time, most people lose this fundamental connection with the pulse of life. The frustration of their basic needs, or even a traumatic event, causes them to hold their breath, tense their muscles and be on their guard against the world.

If your body pulses freely, it becomes a channel for universal and earth energies. You may experience this as love, joy and fulfillment. If you lose the beat, you feel stuck, threatened or even dead. The flow and balance between inner and outer movement, the world within and without, determine the quality of your life. The depth and movement of the breath are good indicators of how harmoniously you are dealing with this polarity in your life.

When you observe yourself or others, you may notice that some people hardly breathe at all. The body seems motionless and is sometimes even dead-looking. If you ask those people how they feel, they say that life is boring or meaningless. Nothing can touch or inspire them. The word inspiration derives from 'inspirare', the inhale or intake of oxygen. Without oxygen there is no joy or excitement.

In a variation on this theme, there are people who breathe somewhat into their belly, but the movement does not reach their chest. The chest looks as if it has collapsed. If you ask those people how they feel, they answer that they feel depressed and sad. The same cause applies: without oxygen, no joyful excitement.

Perhaps you see people who breathe into their chest while their stomach remains flat and motionless. If you take a closer look, you will notice that these people appear to exhale more than they inhale. It is as if they are holding their breath inside. If you ask them how they feel, they answer that life is okay as long as they are in control. If they lose control, they fear that life will overwhelm them. To prevent this happening, they use their brain to keep a grip on existence. These people find it very difficult to exhale fully and surrender to the flow of life.

Another variation are the people who breathe into their stomach and chest, but seem to be willing the movement rather than allowing spontaneous, involuntary respiration to occur. They control the breath rather than allowing it to carry them through life. It is more of a doing than a being, and a further attempt to control the course of life.

In the meantime you may wonder what the movement of breath looks like when it is pulsing in accordance with the rhythm of life. Imagine the breath flowing like a wave through the body. The air enters through the base chakra at the pelvic bottom and fills and rounds out the belly and chest up to the neck. The navel-center rests on the crest of this wave. In the exhale, the navel-center sinks back. The departing breath extends the back and activates and fills the kidneys, the storage place for the life-energy. Then the breath leaves the body through the base chakra and after a short pause, the next wave begins. The flow through the base chakra anchors the body to the ground. In this way, you flow with the events of life without losing your center or your connection with the ground. This practice is recommended as part of one's daily meditation.

If you find it difficult or impossible to physically sense or experience the wave streaming through your body, it may help you to visualize the wave movement that I have just described. Visualization has an immense power to open the doors to the actual physical experience. I tell my clients to use the image of the sea, letting the waves enter the base chakra, fill the whole body, and flow back again in an equal, steady rhythm.

The flow of the movement requires co-ordination and integration. The Basic Pulsation of Life unites in one harmony the four levels of our being: body, feeling, mind and soul. A person whose body vibrates in accordance with this rhythm is free from the pressures of survival and from fears and conflicts. They feel committed to life, deeply connected to the universal mind and at home in their body and on this planet.

## OUT OF TACT

The cultural values and social conditions of our upbringing usually prevent us from developing this harmony within us. Conflicts between our thoughts, feelings and actions interrupt the free flow of energy. We hold our breath, develop muscular tensions and particular body postures, or split the unitary whole into body, mind and soul to cope with cultural or parental demands. This is not a conscious act, rather a reaction to external demands. It protected us against the frustrations, threats and pains which were beyond the coping capacity of the infantile body-mind system. In the course of time, these protective mechanisms became anchored within the physical, emotional and mental systems. Its incarnated power entices the adult to reproduce the frustrations and pains of childhood over and over again.

This dynamic belongs as much to any 'normal' upbringing as to one seared by traumatic events.

In the course of our upbringing each of us hears that certain things are just not done. For example, we may be told in some cultures that we should not strive for things that are out of reach. We are told to be modest and content with what is offered to us. Or we learn that it is not okay to express anger and frustration if we do not get what we want. The impulse to hit out is held back in our arms and shoulders. The built-up tensions make it very hard to reach out for the good things in life, or to receive the beautiful ones.

People with such a block in their shoulders and arms often look as if they are being crucified when they open up their arms towards the universe.

We learn that it is not okay to cry because boys do not do that, or perhaps because it makes our mother feel guilty for not being a better mom. We learn that cute little girls do not get angry, and that it is more important to get good grades in school than to sense, feel or be.

Children are dependent on their parents. They love them and want to please them. So they develop breathing patterns and muscular holding patterns that suppress those feelings that appear unlovable.

**Exercise**

▶ Pay attention to what happens when you are sad or angry:

▷ *Do you suppress these impulses in your throat and so prevent their expression?*

*Do you tighten your chin and press it in to restrict the flow in the throat?*

*Do you tense your arms and shoulders to counter the impulse to hit out?*

*Does mucus develop in your throat? Or does your throat begin to hurt?*

Our everyday language knows of these connections. We speak of 'a voice thick with anger' or 'choked with grief'.

If you have grown up in surroundings where you were constantly asked to suppress your feelings, this restriction becomes programmed into your body. What first served as a protective device to help you retain your parents' love, later on becomes a prison which hinders you from finding love, joy and fulfillment. Because unfortunately not only the oppressive feelings but cheerful ones too are affected by this mechanism.

Or perhaps you grew up in a perfect family which fulfilled all the values and demands of our culture. Like Western culture itself, you will then rate intellectual skills higher than the intuitive or emotional qualities. Like

Western culture, you will see the body as an instrument which must be kept healthy and fit so that it can support the mind at its work. Your energies get directed outwards and upwards. You may flood your brain with so much energy that you cannot stop thinking when you leave work. You may develop the illusion that you can steer and master your life through your brain.

If you belong to this group of people, you are not alone. In the seventies of this century, social scientists discovered the emergence of a new cultural type. According to their description, they, both men and women, maintain a formal distance, are cool, arrogant and shy, but smart. Social status and success attract them. They are avid competitors with a good chance of climbing the career leader.

Compared to their professional capabilities, their private life seems rather meager. They avoid deep feelings and spontaneous impulses and instead prefer a superficial sensuality. They avoid commitment to intimate relationships and isolate themselves. The lack of contact and resulting emotional impoverishment leads to a void within, to fears and depression and a sense that life has lost its meaning. They attempt to escape this painful condition through alcohol, drugs, pills, or working over-time. Reflecting this condition, addiction and co-dependence are the new key-words in the psychological literature.

Intimacy requires that you have a sense of tact. A sense of tact means that you can regulate how close you are to another, or conversely, how distant. This capacity requires that you are in tact with yourself, in-tact with your natural rhythm.

If a person cannot develop his bodily rhythm or his balance, he will find it difficult to feel good around other people. This is especially true of victims of abuse.

In cases of physical or emotional abuse, the personal boundaries were overstepped, shattered or simply could not be built appropriately. People with this background easily absorb the energies of others. They find it difficult to distinguish between themselves and others. For instance, they over-identify with another person and take that person's pain and frustration as their own. Or they approach others and get lost in them. Such people find it difficult, if not impossible, to develop a sense of tact.

In our culture it is rather the rule than the exception to be out of tact. Many people are programmed in tick-tock mode, the rhythm of a clock, which has little to do with our natural rhythm. In tick-tock mode, the natural flow of life changes to calendar pages that are neatly laid out and an artificial rhythm is established in place of the natural sunrise to sunset flow. Tick-tock activates the robot in us and shuts off independent thinking. Tick-tock is the death of curiosity and that urge to explore which has been so much a part of children's lives.

Tick-tock serves all those who want to control people. It does not serve you, not if you want to master your life.

## IN-TACT

How do we manage to be intact? What can we do to find our natural rhythm again, to reconnect with the earth and to bring our physical, emotional, mental and emotional areas into balance?

From my background, the two key elements are breath and grounding. Grounding is a concept derived from Bioenergetic Analysis. It means being rooted in the earth. If the conditions under which you grow up do not make you feel safe, you withdraw your energy from the earth and look for refuge in your mind.

This is a conditioned response. All you need to do is to turn it around. Direct your energy into your navel center and into your feet. Stand up for yourself so that your needs get heard and fulfilled. Place your qualities and abilities where they are needed in the world. Do not run away from painful or difficult situations anymore. Learn to breathe through the pain so that it can change into joy and gracefulness.

Our natural breathing rhythm, the Basic Pulsation of Life, has for most of us been forgone in favor of survival patterns that are supposed to protect us from dangers and injuries. Our best chance of survival, however, is to accept our vulnerability as part of the human condition and return to our basic rhythm.

If you have, up to now, considered your body to be just an instrument of your mind or even an enemy, it is time to befriend your body and carefully nurture it and, if necessary, strengthen its functions or build them up anew. Remember that your body is the vehicle in which you drive through this life. How much care do you lavish on your car? Give your body at least double that attention. Because you cannot just go into the nearest shop and buy a new one.

The strengthening or restructuring of the bodily functions requires daily exercise. The exercises increase your general level of energy. You strengthen the body, develop your self-assertion, set up boundaries in social interactions and examine your perceptions and ideas about the outside world against the reality that the world feeds back to you. The daily practice gives you the self-esteem, strength and power to take charge of your life. Thus, you can create the reality that you wish for.

If your challenge is that you are shielding and bracing your body against the flow of life, then it is more important for you to learn how to let go than to strengthen and rebuild the bodily functions. The chronic muscle tensions and breathing patterns which I described earlier prevent those particular movements which would express your feelings. Feelings are the colors of our lives. Without them life is boring. Allow yourself to take your daily exercise by playfully indulging in those movements that were denied to you in your childhood and adult life. Punch the table, kick your anger out from your neck and shoulders, jump in the air for joy or turn somersaults. Do whatever feels good to you and whatever encourages you to express yourself. It loosens up the body armor, revitalizes the blocked energy and generates that necessary trust for you to surrender to the flow of life.

# Holographic Analysis:
# The Power Of The Images Within

In the section about the Holographic Universe, I pointed out the way in which deeply anchored thoughts and feelings determine our life and future. These thoughts and feelings are mostly unconscious and hidden in the enfolded order of the universe. They originate from experiences in childhood or are patterns brought along from earlier lives or from the collective unconscious. Compared to our adult consciousness, they are immature forms that correspond to an infantile understanding of the situation.

The child interprets events according to the mental capacities and experiences of the particular phase of life when the patterns arose. From the standpoint of an experienced and knowledgeable adult, we may evaluate those situations quite differently. The task is to find an entry point into those patterns that still run our lives today, then understand their function and help them to mature.

The task becomes easier when we understand the properties of such a pattern in terms of a hologram. In a hologram, each part contains the whole. You can call forth the entire picture if you can access one part. This part can be a sensory perception, for instance, the aroma of a meal or a particular sound or the sight of an object or some inner picture. Out of any of these, the overall scene emerges.

For many years I asked myself how I could gain access to the memory bank where the holograms are stored. I asked myself how I could change their nature in such a way that they would lead us to a fulfilled life instead of keeping us in bondage to suffering. In the course of my work, there emerged some core steps which I call the inner alchemy: the transformation of misery into gold. In this process, weakness is new-minted into psychological strength.

## INTUITION

The key to the memory bank lies in your intuitive perceptions which are right brain qualities and which I outlined in the section on 'Self-Realization'. Your intuitive ability allows you to change the dynamic of events. This becomes possible when you grasp the essence of the inner figures of your childhood and preserve their positive function in a more mature form, while releasing their negative aspects.

Intuition may use all the senses. Some people are clairvoyant. They see external happenings with their inner eye. Others are clairaudient and instead of seeing pictures they hear sounds, music or sentences with their inner ear. Others again are made aware predominantly through their bodily sensations, the kinaesthetic sense. Experiences are anchored in the body and can be relived or recovered through physical sensations. And there is a fourth group of people who just 'know'. This is the 'Ah Ha!' effect which vouchsafes insights out of the blue.

All the people I know use intuition in one way or another. Intuition is at work when you, in your living room, suddenly know that the milk is boiling over in the kitchen, or that one of your children is playing the fool, or that the flowers need water. You use your intuitive perception much more frequently than you think. It is just that you do not use it consciously. Or not in the way you expect. Do not fixate on the idea that you must see something in order to get in touch with an inward configuration.

While our senses are bound to the world without, our intuition allows us to enter other dimensions. Depending on your personal philosophy, you may conceptualize these dimensions as something which is outside you, or as something which makes up your deepest core. If you see the universe as a giant hologram or as a conscious space, you become aware that behind our apparent reality there is a deeper layer of which we form part. From our dualistic viewpoint, we first perceive this layer as something outside of ourselves until we become aware of our unity with this deeper level of existence. To use the techniques which follow, it does not matter what is your life experience of this deeper level of being or how you identify it. In Christianity you can call it God, in Buddhism 'Rigpa' or the primordial ground, in quantum physics it is the quantum field, and in general you may call it the universal mind. Although these names come from different traditions, they refer to the same content of fact.

More important still is that you gain access to the level of wisdom and love which characterizes this level of existence. Your inner guide will help you bypass the trickster in your mind and tap into the knowledge which is lying dormant in your unconscious. If the concept of an inner guide feels strange to you, I recommend that you use the temple guide whom you got to know in the section about 'Self-Realization'.

In my sessions with clients I work together with the 'Higher Self', an entity that psychics describe as a light source above the crown chakra. This 'Higher Self' is a bridge between soul and mind. It is an expression of the true self or core of the person. However, if you already feel connected to a wise teacher or an internal figure, use those sources. In the following sections, I will use the term 'inner guide' who can take any shape or form.

## RELAXATION

You find the way to your inner source when you go into the silence. In order to get there, it is important for you to know how to relax. This is not something you can do with your brain. You can use your left brain as a supporter and servant in the process, not as a controller. If you find that you are afraid to get in touch with yourself, practice relaxation techniques first. There are different approaches, such as body work, autogenous training and breathing techniques which offer introductions to meditation.

**Exercise**

▶ Program your unconscious to relax by repeating over and over again the words, "Relax" or "I am relaxed". While saying these words to yourself, breathe deeply and evenly. With each exhale, let go of everything that is on your mind.

I personally prefer the "Inner Smile", a technique that Mantak Chia describes in his book, *Taoist Ways to Transform Stress into Vitality.*[29]

▶ Imagine a smiling face in front of your third eye, and allow that nourishing, warm energy to enter your forehead, eyes and face. Direct this warm stream of energy in three channels through your body. The front channel includes the neck, lungs, heart, liver, kidneys, spleen, pancreas and sex organs, the medium channel the digestive system and the back channel the two halves of the brain and the spine. It is most effective when you manage to enter the organs and systems with your senses instead of just imagining them. So you smell, taste, touch, see or listen to each body part, organ or system through which you direct the energy. With some practice and experience you can let the smiling energy run through the three channels like a waterfall or a shower, washing away all tensions that may be left in the system.

It is worth putting in the time and effort to establish one particular technique for yourself. Then you only to need give your subconscious a signal, and your body and whole being will relax within seconds.

The client usually lies down during a session. It is easier for most people to let go when they are in that position. However, if you are guiding yourself through a session, you may concentrate better if you sit up. Experiment and find out which position serves you best.

I ask my clients to place their hands on their navel-center and focus on their breathing that is moving their hands. Energy follows where you direct

---

29 Chia, Mantak & Maneewan: *Taoist Ways to Transform Stress into Vitality*. Huntington: Healing Tao Books 1985

your attention. You prepare the way for your intuitive perception when you direct your attention away from your mind and towards your navel-center. The navel center unites the conscious and unconscious mind within the

Solar Plexus. The Solar Plexus, situated at the back of the stomach, is the location of the sympathetic nervous system which directs the unconscious, vital processes. The Vagus Nerve connects the Solar Plexus with the particular cerebral region which perceives sense impressions and exercises control over the movements of the body through the cerebrospinal system.[30]

The Solar Plexus is an important energy distribution center. It is like the sun which provides us with light and warmth. If the Solar Plexus is relaxed, it radiates life and vitality into each part of the body.

The more you relax this area, the more energy you radiate to the outside. And the more energy you radiate outside, the more you will pull in events, circumstances and people favorable to your life. You are using the law of attraction which draws together those things, events and people which are on the same vibratory frequency.

### PROTECTION

If your stomach feels tense, breathe into the tension until it loosens up. If you want to deal with a problem which triggers many of your fears and worries, you need to feel safe and calm first. Make sure that you are comfortable and that you feel protected. Sometimes the inner guide will suffice to make you feel safe, sometimes you may need a symbol that gives you protection.

Ask your inner guide for a symbol of protection. Ask about its qualities. If they are positive, let the symbol enter your body and let its energy expand in all directions, from your crown to your toes, until it embraces all body parts. Let the qualities of this energy expand beyond your skin into the electromagnetic field around your body.

This electromagnetic field is also called the aura. It is a vibratory field which surrounds each person. Depending on your radiance, this field can be narrow or wide, whole or rent with holes. If the latter is the case, use the power of a symbol to fill the aura field and close its boundaries. As you experience it in yourself, this may feel like a protection or a sense of security and safety.

---

[30] I owe this information to Leslie Fieger: *The Delfin System*. Alexandra: Delfin International 1995

## THE INNER GUIDE

If my clients are sufficiently relaxed, I ask them to let the inner guide take shape. The guide can take any form, color or configuration. I work with the first picture that comes.

If you have no experience with inner images and do not feel connected to one of the great teachers of mankind, it may help you to imagine a white screen. Ask the inner guide to appear on this screen. The more you are open to letting things happen, the easier is the access to your inner world. Do not attach your expectations to any specific form. The expectation blocks the appearance of the shape, which is important for this session.

I use the image of an adventure trip into unknown terrain. I do not have a clue whom or what I will meet. To go on this journey, I allow myself a curious, neutral interest and the trust that I am led. For this, the inner guide is a necessary precondition.

The guide can take many different forms. He, she or it can appear

- △ as a geometric figure like a triangle, square or circle;

- △ as color points or color clouds;

- △ as a planet, plant or animal;

- △ as a wise figure from a religious or spiritual tradition.

Animal-shapes as wise leaders belong to the tradition of the American Indians. Jesus or Mother Mary come from the Christian heritage, Chinese wise men from the Tao-tradition. You may have a close connection to a currently embodied teacher such as Sai Baba or Mother Meera, who may then appear as your inner guide. Or your guide can be part of your gender (the wise woman or the old, wise man), or belong to different dimensions like angels or fairies. The shape that your inner guide takes usually relates to your beliefs and traditions.

Sometimes the first figures to appear have rather threatening traits, such as monsters, dragons, guards, policemen or soldiers. These creatures usually belong to the issues that you are dealing with. You recognize configurations of the Higher Self through their positive qualities. They are surrounded by an atmosphere of goodness, wisdom and love. They mediate a feeling of protection, safety and security. If you do not get such a feeling, ask your

Higher Self to take shape anew. Or ask the figure whose quality you question whether it is your Higher Self or part of a process that is up for transformation.

In the beginning, the shapes may be indistinct. In the course of time, they take on more concrete forms. If you are very distrustful, the figure can remain distant for a while and only come closer when you start to gain trust. The guide may stay the same for many sessions or change every time. If you have a close connection with a living master, he or she may appear in each session. If the shape changes every time, this may give you a hint about the theme of the session.

The spectrum of the shapes is wide, as wide as the diversity of human experience and too wide to represent them here in detail. Allow yourself to explore and collect experiences. The comforting thing about the inner guide is that you can ask him/her/it about everything. Sometimes the answers take somewhat longer and they come from directions and corners where you least expect them. Do not let yourself be intimidated by this. If you cannot be intimidated, you will understand more easily. Like everything in life, this is also a matter of practice and experience. Remain relaxed and open. Refine your perception and you will learn to understand your images.

Sometimes no shape appears on the screen even though you are relaxed, feel safe and have released all your expectations. If this happens, you should examine whether you really want to look at the matter. Only if you are one hundred percent ready to look at the issues will the information become accessible.

Many people are ambivalent, especially if the issue has to do with traumatic experiences and seemingly insoluble conflicts. Vehement feelings cloud the eye. In such an event, you need another person who will help you to see the situation from a different angle. This may be necessary even if you have had a lot of experience communing with yourself. You come up against your limits, your blind spots that protect you from knowledge which you have not been able to integrate.

Do not start with the most difficult issues. That will just cause frustration, and it hinders your chances of success in the beginning. Start with your bad habits, programmed reactions, bodily symptoms, negative feelings or your resistance to being honest with yourself, and progress from there. If it is feasible for you to work with someone else, explore the techniques together. In the beginning two see better than one.

## TRACKING THE PROBLEM

**Exercise**

▶ Begin by taking responsibility for the problem you want to look at. You can only change something which you have personally created. Describe the situation in as accurate and detailed a way as you can. Ask yourself:

▷ *What is my part in this event?*

*What are my feelings about it?*

*How did I create this problem?*

*Am I willing to change it?*

Let the scene unfold like a play on the stage. Look at all the details from all sides, but beware not to identify yourself with any role or with the event itself. Allow yourself to re-experience the feelings that are connected with the circumstance, but this time as a witness or observer, not as a participant. You need the distance, so that you can see the course of action from a different angle. And you need the connection to the feelings in order to change the problem. Feelings structure the component incidents of an event into a pattern. If you let go of the feelings, the pattern dissolves.

If you have unraveled the event sufficiently, ask it to take shape. The shape sums up all the constituent details into a whole picture. As in the case of the inner guide, the spectrum of the shapes is as broad as the diversity of human experience. The shape that emerges is usually familiar to you and has meaning. Some shapes are physical perceptions, some are inner images. You will find instances among the case examples later in this section.

▶ Have a close look at the shape

▷ *What is its form and color?*

*Do you smell, taste or feel it?*

*Is this shape anchored somewhere in your body?*

*Can your body take on this shape as a posture?*

If you get stuck, ask your inner guide for help. Ask him to show you the appropriate shape, or else help you to keep your distance. Because as soon as you identify yourself with the problem, the problem will dominate you instead of your taking charge of it.

However, if you take responsibility for the situation and your actions and if you have given the whole event a shape, then you are ready for the next important step, which is to shift the pattern from being a problem to becoming an ally.

## THE TRANSFORMATION OF MONSTERS INTO ALLIES

I have spent a large part of my life fighting against the on-going effects of events or situations which have been painful for me. I wanted to get rid of them. I could not understand why this strategy seemed to nourish and strengthen the patterns instead of dissolving them. The more furiously I fought against them, the wilder my resistance became, the stronger they grew. It was like the battle against bacteria and viruses. The stronger the weapons we use to fight and destroy them, the mightier and more refined they become.

It took a long time before I understood that I was putting energy into all the things I was fighting against. Energy follows our intent. If we focus on the things we do not want, we reinforce them. What we want does not emanate from what we do not want. In order to receive what we want, we need to state it and reinforce it.

How then do we deal with the shadow side, with all the events that lie dormant in our unconscious and drive our life from there?

The simplest way is to lovingly embrace this shadow side as part of our experience and human existence. When it is embraced by the light of consciousness, it changes of itself. Negative and positive are the same energy. The energy is connected to one or other pole, and so only appears to be something different.

If you attempt to get rid of the negative, you cut yourself off from a part of your energy source. If you think about intense feelings like anger or grief, you can imagine how much of your energy gets absorbed by such.

A law of the universe states that energy only changes its form, but is not lost. Energy transforms itself, just as water changes into ice or steam. If you think that you got rid of the undesirable, you probably only removed it from your conscious perception, not however from your energy system.

In the unconscious, your wounds and negative thoughts unfold with damaging force. They pursue you like demons or monsters which you no longer recognize as part of you. They appear as something exterior over which you have no influence. If you can recognize that everything, both the good and the bad, are part of the same spirit or consciousness, you can shrink the monsters and use their energy for the productive creation of your life.

How is this possible?

The trick is to transform enemies into allies. If you look at your different idiosyncrasies without judging them, you will see that everything in your reality serves a specific function. They are usually part of basic protective functions like feeling safe in life, or guarding you from harm, violence, disease or isolation.

From an adult perspective, their disadvantage is that they are immature or infantile forms of protection. They have a price. Depending on the developmental stage when they originated, they punish you or control your life. In most people's minds, these burdensome aspects are so much in the foreground that they cannot see the gifts which these quirks bring.

One of my clients had an inner image that she was being squeezed into a crate that gave her hardly any room to move. She sat there with her hands twisted around her bent-up legs and her bowed head pressed against the wooden planking. Just to see what it felt like, we removed the wooden box from her inner image, and to her surprise she found she felt unprotected and unshielded from the outside world. It became clear that the narrow box gave her protection and security, and that she could not simply remove it without first replacing it with another shelter. In a more extended process, we first expanded the box so that she could stand up in it, built in windows so that she could get in touch with the outside world, and finally transformed it into a house which she could enter and leave at her own discretion.

This example demonstrates an essential principle of Holographic Analysis. You cannot just get rid of the limiting patterns. What do you do instead?

First you need to understand the way in which the problem serves you. Then you preserve its useful function in a form which corresponds to your present need and consciousness. In the case of the above-mentioned example, the house fulfills the same protective function as the box, without being a prison. The house gives freedom of movement and the option to use it as needed. Therefore, I suggest you take another look at the 'evils' that make your life miserable. Look with gratitude. Ask yourself:

**Exercise**

▶ What gift does my problem bring me?

What does it give or do for me?

Which important function does it fulfill in my life?

Look at your survival needs, such as your safety and protection from harm, your need for control, warmth, security, stamina, self-worth and dignity. Can you distinguish what need your familiar problem has tried to meet and accept it gratefully?

Be aware that the patterns have developed their own life and may not be ready to give up their existence. You may have nourished them with tears and anger so that they carry a lot of energy. Energy cannot be dismissed, you can only transform it. And you can only transform it if you have completely understood its function and gratefully accepted what it has given to you.

**Exercise**

▶ If you are ready to say goodbye to your familiar program, ask your guide to give you a symbol for its mature form. Examine how you feel with the new shape. Do you feel protected and safe? Do you trust it? Is this shape ready to take on the function of the old program?

Ask it, and pay attention to the answer. The answer can emerge as a picture, a feeling, an inner voice or an inner knowledge. Do not attach yourself to a specific channel of perception. There are many ways to receive an answer.

If your pattern insists that it should remain in spite of your gratitude and willingness to let it go, you may not have yet grasped all of its functions.

A man who had experienced a lot of violence in his childhood felt that violence in his body like a sharp pain in his back. In an inner image, this pain took the shape of a fist. When we looked at this fist more closely, we found that its primary function was to give him the strength to stay upright. We transformed it into a rod that gave him support. However, at this point the fist was not yet willing to give its energy to the rod.

When such a refusal comes up during a session, I ask what is the proportion of the aspect in question in relation to the total function. In this case it was twenty percent. More fundamental than the support was the feeling of power and strength that was connected with this fist. The fist moved him through life, urged him to survive and enabled him to overcome obstacles. The price of such strength was that he could rarely give himself any peace to quietly enjoy life. The constant pressure in his back did not allow him to rest and play. When we understood the dynamic, a solution presented itself which was beyond pressure and self exhaustion. He discovered in himself a detached power that knew when to act and when to rest. This power took the form of a wise guide to whom he could turn for advice.

> If your old survival patterns are unwilling to say good-bye, investigate whether you have grasped all their aspects and use the above example as a model. You reach the point where your old pattern feels acknowledged and is willing to give its energy to the higher form. At this point, you let the old and the new forms come together and watch how the old dissolves into the new.

A woman came to me because her relationships with men habitually failed. She told me that she saw herself in an inner image as a carnivorous plant with a mysterious tube-like pipe that pulled men, especially, into her spell. They wandered in crowds into this fluorescing opening with its hovering luring filaments. Woe to them if they entered. The entrance closed, shark teeth moved out and bit bloody wounds before acid digestive juices began a decomposition process. This plant lived under water in deep darkness without a sense of time. She did not intend to do any evil. She just wanted to survive. She knew no other food than people. That was her nature. Without food she had to die.

The transformation of this organism was surprisingly simple. She turned her innermost to the outside. The long digestive pipe became a stalk, firmly rooted in the ground under the water, and the funnel became a white waterlily with luminous yellow seed-vessels. The luring filaments were transformed into broad carrying leaves on which small creatures dwelt. Now she lives in a field of waterlilies in a calm pond within a small park. She nourishes herself with light instead of darkness, and her beauty pleases the beholders.

The new form functions as a wise consultant to whom you can turn at any time. Make clear with this new shape whether it is ready to teach you all that you need to solve the problem. Make sure that it is committed to your values, such as truth, virtue, peace, love and non-violence. Clarify which specific task your new guide wants to undertake. In the course of time you will build a whole group of mature forms whom you can call together for advice as if sitting around a table. They all have specific functions which will help you achieve what you aspire to in your life.

To achieve this effect, you first need to secure the contact so that this option comes into your mind when you need it. In the beginning, I recommend my clients to arrange a set time for the encounter with the inner guide, and to keep to it. Your old responses still have power and if you do not anchor the new forms firmly in yourself, the old patterns will come back. In general, you need about three weeks of daily contact to make friends with your new guide. Look for the time that suits you best, and then commit yourself to keep this appointment over the next three weeks. With this commitment, you inform your unconscious that you are taking yourself and your well-being seriously. This is an essential step towards success.

## THE RETURN TO CHILDHOOD

Most of the programs that run our life are survival strategies which come from our childhood, and most of them are situations that involve various people. Whenever in your adult life you meet somebody who reminds you, consciously or unconsciously, of an important person in your childhood, you can easily fall back into the feelings or behavior of that time. This is because your old programs function like holograms. You remember the section about the Holographic Universe? Each part contains the message of the whole. Each detail can trigger your old behavior.

If you want to get rid of beliefs and behaviors that are making your life a burden, you need to return to their source of origin. If your soul sees the situation clearly and understands the dynamic, the old program dissolves.

To be able to see clearly, you need to be ready to say goodbye to your familiar story. This has its traps, as I have pointed out in the section about responsibility. For this reason, in the beginning of this work, it helps to get together with a partner. Their task is not to offer you solutions, for the best healer is sitting right inside you. The partner's task is rather to repeat the following questions and to encourage you to look closely and precisely at the past. Their insistence also helps you bring the emerging pictures into focus.

After you have relaxed and got in touch with your inner guide, you ask him/her/it to take you back into the situation which holds the key to the solution of your present problem. This situation may first emerge quite indistinctly. Bring it into the center of your attention by describing what you perceive.

### Exercise

> Describe first of all the environment, and then the child. Look around you:

>> *Where are you?*
>> *What does it look and sound like?*
>> *What is happening around you?*

> Now look at the child. Focus first on the external characteristics.

>> *How old is it?*
>> *What kind of clothes is it wearing?*
>> *What is its posture?*
>> *What is it doing?*

> Then become aware of the expression. Look at mouth and eyes. The expression gives you hints about the emotional state of the child.

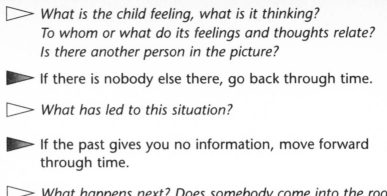

> *What is the child feeling, what is it thinking?*
> *To whom or what do its feelings and thoughts relate?*
> *Is there another person in the picture?*

> If there is nobody else there, go back through time.

> *What has led to this situation?*

> If the past gives you no information, move forward through time.

> *What happens next? Does somebody come into the room?*
>
> *Does the picture of the child change?*

If you are getting no information, you should consider whether the time is right to deal with this issue. You can only see clearly if you are one hundred percent ready. If you are eighty percent ready, then you should work with the remaining twenty. Ask that twenty percent to take shape so you understand where your fears and uncertainties lie. Your resistance is your ally. It gives you hints about the things you may not want to know. Be aware. Your fears and discomforts hold much more power when they are hidden in your unconscious than when you look at them in the daylight.

> If you have a clear picture of the situation and the person involved, you next go into the body of the child. Describe how its body feels.

> *What tensions are you perceiving?*
>
> *Where are the tensions held?*
>
> *Are these tensions familiar to you?*
>
> *What are the feelings and thoughts that are connected with these tensions?*

Be aware. You are an observer and witness of what is happening. Do not identify with the child in this stage. The purpose of this exercise is not that you should blend with the suffering of the child. The point is to understand and recall the feelings which the child experienced at that time. All that your soul needs is the information. This information includes the bodily sensations, the thoughts and the feelings, but not your identification with the event.

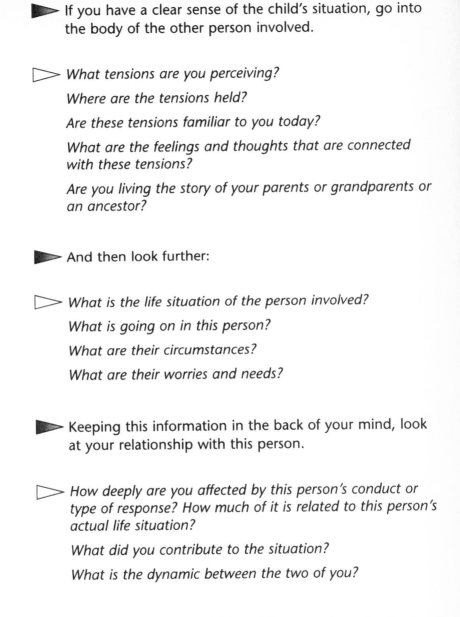

▶ If you have a clear sense of the child's situation, go into the body of the other person involved.

▷ *What tensions are you perceiving?*

*Where are the tensions held?*

*Are these tensions familiar to you today?*

*What are the feelings and thoughts that are connected with these tensions?*

*Are you living the story of your parents or grandparents or an ancestor?*

▶ And then look further:

▷ *What is the life situation of the person involved?*

*What is going on in this person?*

*What are their circumstances?*

*What are their worries and needs?*

▶ Keeping this information in the back of your mind, look at your relationship with this person.

▷ *How deeply are you affected by this person's conduct or type of response? How much of it is related to this person's actual life situation?*

*What did you contribute to the situation?*

*What is the dynamic between the two of you?*

You may find it odd that you should be able to go into the body of another person and perceive what is happening there, or grasp the circumstances of their life. In the beginning of this work I was astonished how easily my clients could access this information and what a wealth of data they brought back from those inner journeys. This is not so amazing to me anymore, when you consider that children protect themselves from adults by 'reading' their moods and intentions, especially in threatening situations.

In the beginning, I was also surprised to find that almost all my clients recognized the other involved person's tension pattern in themselves. Only when I started to conceive the universe as a holographic unit did this make sense to me. Energetically, we are all interrelated. In consequence, children take on the postures and attitudes of their parents energetically, especially in situations that represent incisive experiences for them.

From psychology we have the concept of the 'identification with the aggressor'. This states that, in order to protect ourselves, we identify with somebody who attacks us. This process is not only a psychological mechanism. It is an energetic process. It affects us in that we carry on the same patterns from generation to generation. Whole generational chains get produced and transmitted in this way. I consciously use the term 'transmission' here because these programs are anchored energetically in our body-mind system. However it is possible to interrupt these chains by cutting the ties.[31]

In a young woman's inner image this generational chain presented itself as a tapeworm which had gnawed deep into her heart and twined itself around parts of her stomach and liver. It had poisoned the inner source and everything which it encompassed. Every single piece of it bristled with barbs and each had to be carefully removed so that no fiber remained from which a poisonous new worm could grow. After the laborious 'operation', the inner source bubbled forth clearly.

## THE RELEASE OF TENSION PATTERNS

If you have arrived at the point where you see the situation clearly and can understand the dynamics, the question then arises whether you are ready to let it go.

At this point I ask my clients to imagine a figure of eight. Each of the persons involved stands in one of the circles. I ask them to let the two circles move apart until they are a good distance from each other. The two separated circles symbolize the ability to perceive the 'other' as separate from oneself. This ability develops in the course of our first three years of life.

---

[31] I owe this term and the idea of the figure of eight to a seminar with Phyllis Crystal. See also her book: *Cutting the Ties that Bind: Growing Up and Moving On.* Samuel Weiser 1994

If both circles overlap or touch each other and are not able to move apart, it means that the inner child has not yet separated sufficiently from the parent to establish its own identity. If such is the case, the following technique is not suitable. It is then more advisable to first strengthen and mature the inner child.

**Exercise**

▶ Imagine a figure of eight. Let both circles move away from each other, so that they are a comfortable distance apart. Establish clear boundaries and put yourself and the other person each in one circle. Describe how both people look now.

▷ *Are you still a child or are you an adult?*

*What is the position of the two people in respect to each other? Do they face each other or are they looking away?*

*What does the expression on their faces tell you about the feelings they have for each other?*

▶ If the relationship between them is clear, ask your inner guide for a shape that represents the tension pattern and its associated feelings and thoughts. Take the picture that first comes to your mind. Give this shape back to the circle of the other person. The other person will usually accept it if the course of events was part of his or her personal responsibility. He or she will refuse it if you are dealing with a generational chain. In that case, give the shape to your inner guide.

The release may feel as if a mountain has dropped away from you. At the same time you are losing a burden that has become familiar. In some cases the removal of the old pattern feels as if it has left you with a deep wound. In this case ask your inner guide to close the wound, or to give you a balm with which you can purify and cure the hurt. The removal of such a dynamic is often like a major operation. If you feel exhausted, give yourself time to recover.

One of the principles of this work is that you cannot remove anything from the energy system without substituting something for it. The substitute is the symbol of a pure energy. Depending on the situation, this symbol can come from a good figure like the inner guide, or from the person involved.

You will find instances of this in the case example section which follows.

## PARTING

When you are ready to let go of the shadow of the past, then the time for parting has come. In respect to the important figures from childhood such as parents, you do not say goodbye to your actual father and mother but to the images that you have carried over from childhood. The same principle applies as that which I introduced for transforming a pattern. You can only let go of somebody if you can let them go in gratitude.

**Exercise**

▶ Ask your inner guide for a symbolic gift which you can offer to the other person as a sign of your new understanding. With it, you express your willingness to let go of the old situation. To fulfill its purpose, your gift must clearly appreciate the other person. Check the qualities of the symbol. If they are all positive, you offer it to the person in the other circle.

If your counterpart is not used to being treated kindly, he or she may respond with surprise and hesitation. Do not withdraw at this point. In my experience, a pure gift is always accepted in the end and induces relief and gratitude in the other person. Frequently, I experience that people with whom contact has been broken off for years will pick up the phone after this moment of reconciliation. The work within has an effect without.

▶ After you have delivered your gift, ask the other person in return for a present which signifies their pure love or intent. This souvenir comes in symbolic form. Examine its qualities, so that you are sure that it is a pure gift signifying their love, acknowledgment, appreciation or caring. Let the symbol enter your body so that it can become anchored in your energetic system. The power of this symbol replaces the tension pattern which you dissolved earlier.

If you are dealing with a parent whom you do not want to forgive, you should consider two points.

Your parents have given you life. They are not obliged to do anything else. It is your responsibility what you make out of the circumstances of your life.

Parents are people and like all people, they have their weaknesses. Often, because of the personal challenges in their life, they may not have been in a position to transmit their love and care to their children in the ways they might have wished. If you have children yourself, you know that parents often know their own weak points and suffer from the knowledge. Give them the chance to express their positive intentions on the inner planes, and give yourself the opportunity to replace the old tensions with a nourishing shape.

When my clients take in and anchor the new shape, many of them experience a feeling of relief and satisfaction. In cases where relationships have been full of conflict, they feel satisfied that they can finally make peace with their story. Give yourself time to experience these feelings. Let the symbolic gift continue to fill you and impart what you may have missed all your life. Then this gift will become a positive power that strengthens and nourishes you and reconciles you with the past.

> At the end of the session, say goodbye to the person in the other circle. Let his or her circle begin to move away towards the horizon. Observe how the circle becomes smaller and smaller and finally disappears beyond the horizon. Thank your inner guide for his guidance. And nurture yourself and give yourself time. Be aware that this work can be at least as deep and affective as a serious physical operation. Be good to yourself in the days following. Give yourself time to recover and to anchor the new experience.

## THE UNFOLDED SELF

In many cases it is helpful to first try out and become familiar with the new shape in your inner world. With trust in your newly gained power, it will be much easier to utilize your new insights and behavior in actual situations. We know from research that sportsmen who predominantly use their imagination to prepare themselves for a competition achieve better results than sportsmen who train every day.[32]

For this next step you need either the matured shape of your old pattern or the gift from your childhood partner. You can add this step directly to the work that I described in the sections about 'The Transformation From Monsters To Allies' and 'Parting', or do it separately at your convenience. In the latter case you should start with relaxation before bringing the matured shape or the gift into focus.

**Exercise**

▶ Put your hands on your navel-center and allow your breath to move your hands. Let go of all your thoughts and ask your Higher Self to take shape.

Ask for the emergence of the matured shape of your transformed problem or the symbolic gift of your childhood partner. Let it enter your body. Fill yourself with its qualities and let the energy of those qualities expand beyond the body boundaries and fill your aura, which is the electromagnetic field around you.

Become all these qualities. Ask yourself:

▷ *How does it feel for my body to be this shape, this symbol?*

*What do I feel, now that I have this new shape?*

*What thoughts are going through my head?*

*What is important to me in this new shape? What really matters in my life?*

---

[32] Compare Michael Talbot: *The Holographic Universe*. New York: HarperCollins 1991

▶ Give this shape time to fully unfold in you. Within your imagination, this can take days, weeks, months or years. Travel forward through time until you become one with this new form.

And then, as this figure, go out into the world. Watch for the situation which comes up first in your imagination. It can be something familiar or unfamiliar. Just be aware and watch how the world meets you as this new shape. Ask yourself:

▷ *How do I feel around other people, or in my environment? How do I feel if I live up to my full potential?*

▶ Give yourself time to let the scene unfold fully. Pay attention to details, to thoughts, feelings and interactions. If further situations emerge, let them pass you by like a pictorial broadsheet. Focus on what the pictures have in common. What does the broadsheet want to tell or show you?

▶ Look back from this point in the future to your current situation and the person who you are now. What is different? What has stayed the same?

How powerful is the tension between these two pictures?

The tension is structural and not psychological in nature. If the tension seems so great that you feel frightened or get in a panic, ask your inner guide to show you that level of your realized potential which is appropriate to you now.

Put both scenes, your future picture and your current situation, into two circles which are a good distance apart from each other. Imagine that both circles are connected by an elastic band. Allow your full potential Self to pull the picture of your current reality effortlessly to itself until both circles become one.

In your own time, return to your room as this new shape.

If you have anchored the new figure in your body, you can use it to go through difficult or threatening situations in your mind before you have to deal with them in reality. You will notice that merely the trial runs will change the actual situations in such a way that you can deal with them in much more relaxed fashion.

## CONNECTING TO THE INNER CORE: A CASE EXAMPLE

I would like to illustrate the principles which I have described by recounting an actual session. The theme of this session was the client's move to another country. That also meant deep changes in respect of living place, work and relationships. Marianne did not yet know what to expect in her new environment. The unknown future frightened her and triggered feelings of homelessness and lack of direction. These fears expressed themselves as chest pains.

There were two dreams that were closely connected to this situation. In the first dream she was in a many storied house which had many people but no roof. The hail just pounded through. In the second dream she was a passenger in a car which was driving through the streets backwards.

1.  We start with relaxation. I direct her attention towards her Solar Plexus and then ask her to let her Higher Self take shape.

    *"It's an onion."*

    *"Aah, many layers, beautiful. We would like to get to the core."*

    I regard the onion as a hint to move through the different layers until we reach the core. And in fact, before we arrive at the core of the problem, Marianne's Higher Self guides us first through the different aspects of the images which follow.

2.  She notices a severe pain in her heart chakra..

    *"How does the pain feel?*

    *"Like an open wound..."*

    *"Ask the pain to take shape."*

*"It looks like a V or a valley. It narrows towards its end. It is dark there and it looks as if there is a cave underneath with a lot of red and orange inside. There is some cooking going on inside, and it looks as if there are many wires lying around that are all disconnected. It's a big mess."*

Pain is somewhat abstract and often inconceivable. If we let the pain take shape, we open up the possibility of decoding its message. In Marianne's first image there is much fire and chaos, which corresponds to her momentary emotional state. Her emotional state also gets expressed in her next image, in which she sees herself in a desperate frame of mind, abandoned in the desert.

3.     *"Ask the onion to show us what the situation is all about."*

*"I am in a desert. I feel kind of lost in this large empty plain. In the distance I see a point. It looks like an opening. I am alone and I feel as if I am the only one to have survived a catastrophe."*

*"Describe what you look like."*

*"I am a strange creature with large black eyes, like a squirrel but with tough scales instead of fur. Next or parallel to me there is a person in armor, like in a moon-landscape."*

*"A kind of astronaut?"*

*"Yes."*

*"Are there one or two people?"*

*"Two. They stand side by side and look in the same direction."*

*"Describe the landscape. What does it look like?"*

*"White, like snow or sand or dust."*

*"Is the black point still there?"*

*"Yes, it is now a cave which belongs to the little creature."*

*"Go into the little creature."*

*Marianne, surprised...* *"It feels itself at home there. It does not know anything else."*

*"Oh! Does it feel good?"*

*"Yes, very good. It is one with this landscape and the cave, it feels safe and it is at one with itself. It lacks nothing, it is content."*

*"It has precisely what you lack?"*

*Marianne, surprised... "Yes."*

Marianne's attitude and her interpretation of the image is first directed towards some danger, a threat or even a disaster. The development of the image shows that the issue does not have to do with something bad as originally suspected. The little creature owns something which she is missing: safety, a home and an anchor.

In your sessions, beware of leaping too fast to conclusions. Often the images unfold in a direction completely different to that originally assumed. The little creature, which at first sight seemed so unattractive, turns out to be a stable core which is at peace with itself and at one with its world.

4.　　　*"Fine. Now ask the little creature to enter your body and expand there, and tell me where it enters."*

*"... in the heart..."*

*"Fine. Let it fill the wound in the heart and spread out from there."*

I give her time to direct the energy through the different parts of her body and in this way fill herself with the sense that she is at home.

*"The energy does not go through my arms."*

*"Aha, what kind of feeling is that?"*

*"Like a resistance."*

*"Let the resistance take shape."*

*"It is an agave plant with thorny leaves that are pointed outwards."*

*"What is its message?"*

*"Don't come too close."*

*"And how does the agave feel about that?*

*"On the one hand fine, because she can keep people off her skin, but on the other hand she also needs water."*

*"That sounds like a dilemma. She would like both attention and distance, and does not know how to get both at the same time?"*

*"Yes, that is how it feels. This dilemma is familiar."*

I understand the agave to express her need for protection. She shields herself from other people. Simultaneously she also needs attention. The question is, how she can set safe boundaries for herself and at the same time receive care.

5.      *"Let's have a closer look at the astronaut. Go into his body and describe what you perceive."*

*"He is stuck in his armor. He can only look straight ahead."*

*"His field of vision is constricted?"*

*"Yes. For example, he cannot see the little creature. He looks into the distance."*

*"Oh! So he feels safe in his armor?"*

*"Yes, very. He does not have any feelings, but only a scientific sort of head."*

*"Does it seem as if he is quite fearless because his attention is completely focused on the view in the distance?"*

*"Yes, he is totally fixed on the idea of survival."*

I interpret the astronaut as the brain or mind which is completely fixed on survival. He is so narrow that he cannot see the little creature. When I direct his attention to it, he makes fun of the little creature and slanders it. It turns out at the end of the session that denial and ridicule of the little creature, which is Marianne's inner core, is part of the family story. In consequence, she has lost the connection to her core being, her inner guide. This is not an uncommon finding. To re-establish the connection, I ask the positive aspects which come up during a session, like the little creature, to enter the body. Often, this is not as simple as it sounds. Some body parts refuse to let the energy come through, or they are so blunted that at first they cannot take it in.

6.  *"Okay, let's take care of the wires from the first image."*

   *"Yes, somehow we must knit those wires together."*

   *"Ask the onion if this is correct. Have the wires become useless in the course of time because they have fulfilled their purpose? Can we simply clear them out?"*

   *Marianne asks her Higher Self and tells me in surprise,"Yes, that is right. They are left over from my past. I do not need them anymore."*

   *"Fine. We send the little creature into the heart cave and ask it to use its scaly armor to clear the cave out."*

   *(After a short while)*

   *"There are still more in my pelvic cave."*

   *"Fine, then we let the little creature continue there. Ask it to clear everything out and to stack it in a big pile, so that we get rid of the old junk."*

The little creature stacks up the wires in a big pile outside the body.

   *"Ask this pile for its gift."*

   *"It gives me a sense of the pain and suffering of all human beings and mankind, all the terror and the fear of many generations."*

   *"Ha! So that connects you with mankind?"*

   *"Yes."*

   *"See whether we should burn the pile or whether you need it as a link to your humanness and the fate of mankind."*

   *She ponders the question. "I need the wires as a link."*

   *"Fine, then we build an archive next to the cave, the library of mankind so to speak, with a large door and a key that gives you*

*access whenever you want without being overwhelmed by the suffering."*

She is happy about the archive and feels relieved.

Many people think that it is necessary to clear everything up, processing things through to the very end, as Marianne did in regard to the wires. The solution is often much simpler and has to do with your ability to release things. If you understand, value and accept an event's positive function, the soul frees itself from the burden of the experience and preserves the learning result. Only this learning result is important. It does not matter how you acquire it. You can attain it through pains and disappointments, or with lightness, joy and gratitude. How you choose has to do with your cultural conditioning.

In Marianne's case, the wires connect her to the collective fate of mankind, the history of our pain and suffering. This link guarantees belonging and humanness. For this reason, we are preserving the experience in the archive. She can go there whenever she needs, without risk of being overwhelmed or having the suffering run her life.

7.  In the next picture the landscape emerges under a thick layer of dust.

    *"The whiteness is like a layer of dust which is lying on the land-scape. One can blow the dust away."*

    *"What does the landscape look like?"*

    *"It's green like a place I know from my home town, with a view over the lake to the mountains. It's really corny that this lake shows up over and over again."*

    *"That is your home, and you have not made your peace with your home. What lies beyond the place?"*

    *"The sea."*

    *"Okay, then let's see what your new cave must look like."*

Here I am alluding to the move and her new place of residence.

    *"Detached, with a lot of space and light, where I can be with people who teach."*

    *"Would you like to learn from them?"*

After we have linked her to her humanness, the landscape becomes visible under the thick layer of dust. It is her native place to which she feels connected and at the same time wants to move away from. She has given up her apartment and must now find a new home. Her longing is pulling her to a place with much light and warmth, a place where she can find peace and commune with herself.

8.        *"My whole resistance is coming up."*

*"What does your resistance say?"*

*"You do not need to learn from others. You can do it by yourself."*

*"Who says that?"*

*"My father."*

*"Let this voice take shape."*

*"It is like a shiny, sharp dagger which cuts through everything."*

*"What does the little creature do with it?"*

*She laughs..."It sews a slip-cover for the dagger, with holders so that it can pull the cover behind it and the dagger cannot cut it."*

*"What does it want to do with the slip-cover?"*

*"It uses it as a slide and a seat."*

We both laugh. The little creature has a lot of playful wit.

Her family history does not allow her to find the place of inner peace. The resistance gives you important hints on how you have learned to survive. Consider the resistance as an ally and not as an enemy.

Her father dissected everything with his mind, like the astronaut in the beginning of the session. So the mind became a weapon which turned against her. She must first of all neutralise this weapon by sewing the cover, then use it as a support (seat) and learn to deal with it playfully (the slide). But in Marianne's case, the resistance has a paternal and maternal component.

9.       *"Can you imagine that for the next ten weeks you could sit on the seat dagger for half an hour each morning and evening and talk with the little creature?"*

*"I would like to, but I have too much resistance."*

*"What does this resistance say now?"*

*"I only do what I want to do. I do not allow anybody to pin me down."*

*"To whom are you saying that?"*

*"To my mother."*

*"Give this resistance a shape."*

*"A silver thistle, totally sharp and thorny."*

*"What is the gift?"*

*"Freedom."*

*"Yes. That is the rebellious child who asserted itself against the mother and in this way built up its identity. The problem is though that this form of self-assertion hinders you from getting what you really want."*

*She nods thoughtfully and approvingly.*

*"Ask your onion to show you a mature form of your need for self-assertion."*

*"A pomegranate with many different seeds, differentiated and yet bound into a system."*

*"Fine. That is you with all your different characteristics. Now we have reorganised the chaos which we found at the beginning."*

The second form of resistance, the silver thistle, originates from the relationship with the mother. It belongs to the time when one's identity gets formed. The shape is tied up with the infantile rebellion, with saying 'no'. It does not allow her to use this same power to say 'yes', to create her own life. So we mature it. The pomegranate is an integrated form, which contains all the kernels, which equal subpersonalities, and encloses them within a clearly defined shell. The chaos of the wires has changed into a new form.

10.        *"And what shall I do with the dagger?*

*"We will wait until your contact with the little creature is so good that you can use this dagger, or the mind, for your own good. Your father used it to cut off all connections and, in taking this dagger on, you cut yourself off from your inner core. When the time is ripe and you can handle this dagger, you can use it to open up your way in life. In order to do that, you must work with these symbols so that your inner world can form itself into a new structure."*

*"How should I do that?"*

*"You talk with the little creature every day, and while you do that you sit on the heritage of your father, the domesticated dagger that is in the slip-cover, and you hold the pomegranate in your hand."*

*"I would feel silly and ashamed to do something like that."*

*"Okay. Then we do a test dialogue, and you tell the little creature everything you are feeling at the moment."*

In an internal dialogue she expresses both positions, that of the little creature and that of her resistance.

*"Okay, little creature, I find it absurd to talk with you."*

*"I feel that, and I understand it. Your parents did not see me. You can find it absurd, yet I will talk with you. I will ask you questions and you can answer."*

*"Yes, that is okay. What should we talk about?"*

*"You can tell me about your night-time fears, if you like."*

*"Fine, and what then?"*

*"I can ask you what your day looks like, and you can tell me your ideas. Then I will tell you what I would like to do and we will see how they match."*

*"Fine, that is a useful suggestion. I am ready to try that."*

The last step is a trial run with the goal of overcoming the parental block regarding the little creature. To change something in life, we ultimately must do it.

## DEALING WITH TRAUMATIC EVENTS

Sometimes the event has been so serious and so deeply hurtful that you do not want to go back into it without the assistance of another person. One of these painful areas is sexual abuse, which has drawn a lot of attention in recent times. Over the past few years I have worked with many people who were confronted in one way or another with this kind of trauma during their childhood. Out of this work have come some other techniques, for which I recommend you to have someone else to assist you initially. With some experience, you can use them by yourself.

Abuse is an attack on one's emotional and physical integrity, an abandonment or even an assassination of the soul. When there is a continuous or a traumatic attack on one's personal integrity, the soul reacts by retreating, freezing or splitting. The body-mind unit, which is symbolized in the figure of the centaur, splits into a horseman. The rider is the mind and the horse is the body.

The body becomes an object of shame, especially if it felt pleasure, which is its natural response to sexual stimulation. Because of the traumatic circumstances, the mind cannot tolerate the pleasure response of the body. It cuts itself off from it and takes the lead. Instead of the body, the mind becomes the basis of identity. It rides the body into the ground out of shame, guilt and self-punishment. The mind does not recognize this behavior as self-destructive, especially if, to escape its pain and loneliness, it is supported by our culturally accepted pleasure cravings such as smoking, alcohol, pill consumption, and work-, sex- or relationship addictions.

Several steps are necessary to work through this situation and cure the split between body, mind and soul. First, one needs to mature the body- and ego-functions and to set up healthy boundaries that were overstepped during the abuse. To do this, the body needs to be prepared to become the basis of identity. This is done by liberating it from the stigma of the abuse.

The body is held especially responsible for the event if it felt pleasure. For the clients, this is the most difficult aspect. The fragile ego feels menaced by the body's neediness or pleasure drives which threaten to overwhelm it. As a consequence, the body is to be seen as dirty, unreliable or hostile and must therefore be punished or at least held in chains, especially in cases where bulimia or anorexia serve as coping mechanisms.

To set the body free from all guilt, I choose a ritual, symbolic bath. I ask the client to imagine a brook, a lake or a waterfall, and to immerse themselves in it until the body is freed from all dirtiness.

As a further step, I separate the energy system of the victim from that of the abuser. For this I use the same procedure as I described in the section about the release of physical tensions. When this has been done, the mind and the soul are usually willing to accept the body as an equal partner in negotiations, and I begin with a restructuring between the three parts.

Usually, the mind has taken over responsibility for the safety of the abuse victim and for this reason has taken the dominating role. Morally, the mind condemns the body and holds it responsible for the event. I explain to the mind that the body functions according to the principles of pleasure and displeasure, and not according to moral values. I propose to the mind that it makes the soul the leader of the body-mind-spirit unit and that it uses its sharp perceptions to support the soul. We arrange that the soul and the mind together nourish the body and support its development. Under these conditions, the soul generally declares itself ready to return to the body and fill it with its life force, after we have cleansed it from disgrace and shame.

The return happens in a symbolic way. I ask the soul to take shape and enter the body. Then I make sure that the life energy fills all parts of the body. This can take a considerable time because often the whole body, or parts of it, are quite numb. Often, I ask the client to imagine that there are pipes running through the blocked joints, and that through these the energy can move.

In the next step I discuss how the clients can take care of their body and rebuild its functions. In the case of eating disorders, I make concrete agreements for dealing with food. On the inner plane, I use the 'inner smile', the technique that Mantak Chia brought to the West. It brings relaxation, warmth and strength to the body. I have outlined this technique in the section about relaxation.

Successful negotiations are a key factor in the client's preparedness to do the daily work which is necessary to heal the abuse. The new balance between body, mind and soul is an essential requirement for the maturation of the organism.

Successful negotiations are comparable to peace negotiations between hostile troops. Perseverance and skill are necessary to keep the three parts in dialogue with each other. The therapist is the mediator who understands the different viewpoints and their separate languages, and who acknowledges them for the contributions they have made towards handling an impossible situation.

The construction of an integrated identity can take many years, depending on the degree of disturbance. One needs to develop a certain strength before one can look at one's life-story from the viewpoint of the soul contract, and release the feelings, pains and limitations that one had to confront as a consequence.

If we have worked long and deeply enough, we reach the point discussed in the last section of 'Self-Realization', which I have called the 'choice point' between drama and joy. Here we have the choice, either to continue to feel miserable or to transform weakness and deficiency into psychological strength. By choosing the latter, we can support others who are undergoing a similar fate.

# Holographic Repatterning: The Law Of Resonance

### BODY, MIND AND SOUL AS A VIBRATORY FIELD OF RESONANCE

In the section about 'The Cycle of Manifestation' I pointed out that we can trace our thoughts, feelings and physical processes back to the functioning and interplay of the five elements. These five elements, Ether, Air, Fire, Water and Earth, are the names given to specific qualities of energy and consciousness. The five elements are the expression of an underlying pulsating energy field which is the basis of all life. With its pulsating movement of expansion and contraction, it creates wave patterns that energize, vitalize and shape our physical processes, organs and systems, and our thoughts, feelings and behaviors.

Each wave pattern has a frequency. In physics, frequencies are measured in cycles per second. Each organ in the body has a different frequency which guarantees its optimal functioning. We use this knowledge when we balance and harmonize the body-mind system by using healing sounds.

Our senses also perceive everything in our environment in terms of frequencies. We see, hear, smell, taste and touch in frequencies, though only within a certain range. For instance, we hear only waves that run from 16-20,000 cycles per second. The squeak of the bat escapes most people aged over forty. We see no skeleton as do X-rays, and our eye is unable to discover radioactive radiation. Some poisons escape our sense of smell, and smokers know how their sense of taste is restricted to less than normal range. All frequencies affect us in our life, even if we do not record them with our conscious senses.

If you are flowing with life, your body-mind system vibrates at its optimal frequency. In the section about 'The Basic Pulsation Of Life' I described the feelings and awareness that accompany such an optimal resonance. You feel connected with the earth, its people and the universe, and you experience this as love, joy and fulfillment.

For most people, the Basic Pulsation of Life became disrupted or blocked at some point by the circumstances of their lives. They hold their breath, armor their muscles, or even let themselves die. The body responds to these imbalances with tensions, symptoms and finally disease. The soul and emotional body may experience pain, depression, conflicts, work-difficulties, unhappy relationships, or a general sense of being dragged down and unable to feel happy and joyful.

If all these symptoms and states of stress and unhappiness can be traced back to frequency wave patterns, this means that we can change the specific configuration. This is as simple as finding the right station on the radio or television – if you know how to do it. If you twist the dial on the radio, all you are doing is changing frequencies. All we therefore need is a system like radio or television which provides us with this option.

Chloe Wordsworth has very eloquently put together such a system in a six step process. She combines a broad spectrum of traditional and modern healing modalities in an elaborate system that helps identify those aspects of our body-mind system that have lost their optimal frequency, and checks for those self-healing techniques that will help it regain its optimal functioning.[33]

You can either learn the procedure for yourself within three weekend seminars, or you can go to a qualified practitioner to help you through the difficult areas and questions in your life, or you can register for a course where a qualified practitioner will shift the frequency of a specific theme for a whole group.[34]

---

[33] Among them are Polarity therapy, Chinese acupuncture, Edu-Kinesiology, the Japanese Jin Shin harmonising points, Indian Yoga practices and work with sound-frequencies.

[34] You will find references at the end of the book.

The next section gives you an overview of the six step process followed by an explanation of the procedure.

## THE SIX STEP PROCESS [35]

### *1. Preparation*

The first step of the six step process deals with our willingness to improve or expand our life. We only change if we are ready to change. This sentence is not as prosaic as it sounds. Our mind or our will are often moving ahead while our emotions are holding us back.

A deep change will only happen if our whole system is ready and our thoughts, feelings and will are aligned to solve the problem. Sometimes, despite our expressed intention, we may not be ready to look at and change our life-depleting strategies. In such a case, we need to attune our body-mind to use the session to the best of its ability.

### *2. Motivation*

We change only if we are motivated to change. The second step deals with those motives that cause us to seek help.

As long as we are attached to suffering, the impulses to make changes stem predominantly from that area. Most people move along a chosen path until external forces change their direction. Generally these externals are diseases, separations, losses, unemployment or homelessness, circumstances which painfully and decisively change the course of life. If you understand these events correctly and act upon them positively, however difficult or painful they are, they have the potential to awaken you and turn your whole life in a new direction.

External events mostly motivate a person to seek help and support. In the sessions we discover that these occasions are the catalyst for deeper material. The original problem often serves as an entry point to a longer journey of discovery into one's Self. In these sessions, a whole web of less conscious interrelated issues may come up and shine a new light on the old and familiar ones.

---

[35] Chloe Wordsworth and Anthea Becker have summed up the work in two booklets which I use as reference. Compare Chloe Wordsworth: *Holographic Repatterning. Model and Process for Positive Change and Transformation.* 1994 and Anthea M. Becker: *Holographic Repatterning Handbook.* 1994. To receive both pamphlets and information about seminars and practitioners of Holographic Repatterning, contact: HR Sales. 6770 W. Hwy. 98A-# 50, Sedona, AZ 86366. USA. Tel. 001-520-204 9960, fax 001-520-204 9905; email: hrsales@sedona. net

### 3. Positive Intentions

The second kind of motivation to change is part of the positive intention to grow through joy, in other words to unfold our potential. We express this desire through a positive intent or affirmation of what we would like to achieve.

An affirmation is composed of consciously chosen words which express or support your intention. An example is, "I am loving" or "I am healthy and vital." Affirmations give your energy a positive goal.

Affirmations delete old programs and replace them with new ideas, insights and objectives. A client who was finding pleasure in her failures changed her viewpoint with the affirmation, "I am a success". Another client whose life was determined by a fear of falling, which had escalated to a phobia for moves and changes, altered her life's perspective with the sentence, "I move actively towards positive change and growth."

Your feelings or actions often sabotage your best intents because they function on a lower frequency level than the situation you desire. You can wish for health and at the same time be attached to junk food. You can long for a good partnership and at the same time be full of hostility and mistrust towards the other sex.

Holographic Repatterning shifts your frequency back to its optimal level of functioning in respect to your positive intention, so that all levels of your being are united and attuned towards the same goal. If you are in harmony with your ideals, your life moves continuously towards realization of those ideals.

### 4. Unconscious Patterns and Energy Restrictions

The fourth step deals with those unconscious patterns which support your limiting strategies and prevent you from realizing your positive goals.

Holographic Repatterning works with three fundamental types of un-conscious patterns:

△ Beliefs which are reflected in your self-image and language;

△ Survival strategies which helped you overcome traumatic situations, but today hinder you from living a fulfilled life;

△ Energy constrictions in your Element, Meridian and Chakra systems.

We will deal with each of these areas in turn.

We are what we think. And above all, we are what we have heard and experienced from our environment, principally parents, teachers and media. This nexus of opinions, judgments and prejudices determines how we see and create reality. If these opinions are negative, less than optimal frequencies run our life. We have then limited our ability to manifest a positive reality. Only if we transform the underlying structures can we reach a permanent change which allows us to unfold our full potential.

Survival mechanisms are anchored in our animal part, the brain stem. From there, they direct our reaction to current situations which carry reminders of earlier traumatic events. Our animal part responds to danger with a flight-fight mechanism. If circumstances do not allow expression of the appropriate response, we hold the blocked energy in our brain. As a result, we may withdraw when confronted with threatening situations; or we may become paralyzed, isolate ourselves, or get into a panic; or use violence, force and control mechanisms. These programmed reactions prevent us from recognizing possible sources of danger and responding to them appropriately. Nor are we able to relax in the certain trust that our survival needs and safety are taken care of. Holographic Repatterning anchors useful and life-enhancing reactions in the brain and nervous system.

The third area which prevents us from living a fulfilled life are the blocks or constrictions in the energy centers and flow lines of our body-mind system.

In the section called 'The Cycle of Manifestation' I have described how, according to the Ayurvedic system, the five elements of Ether, Air, Fire, Water and Earth govern our physical functioning, emotional states and mental attitudes. Traditional Chinese medicine determines our well-being by using the five elements of Wood, Fire, Earth, Metal and Water and the associated meridians or energy flows in the body. For example, the earth element controls the nurturing, supportive aspect and relates to our security and grounding. If this element is blocked, our legs may feel uncertain, we may make ourselves at home in our mind instead of in our body, or have the sense that we cannot receive the physical, emotional or mental food that we need.

Using Holographic Repatterning, you can identify the energy constrictions in your system and how they affect particular areas of your life. These areas can relate not only to your personal life, such as your body, feelings or thoughts, but to your relationships, work situation or connection with the universe.

Unconscious responses relate to unresolved earlier experiences in which basic life or spiritual needs were not met. Some of these situations are just part of the cycle of life, such as when siblings are born, when parents move and you have to change school and friends, or when parents separate. Others are of a traumatic nature such as witnessing a fatal accident, or experiencing the abuse of power in one of its many ways, or the loss of loved ones. Some of these events may be prenatal experiences or unresolved issues of an archetypal nature. They connect us with the collective unconscious of mankind. To resolve these situations, you only need to bring forth those aspects of the past event which are having a determining effect on your present life.

### 5. Self-healing Modalities

Chloe Wordsworth has put together a broad variety of self-healing techniques derived from western and eastern traditions. Among them are body movements, breath techniques, acupuncture, toning, overtone chanting, tuning fork vibrations, light frequencies, creative expression and affirmations.

In these sessions you use a muscle checking technique to identify the sources of energy which your body-mind system needs in order to regain its optimal functioning in respect to the issue at hand. I will explain this in the next section.

### 6. Positive Action

Sometimes, it takes more than just one session to return to the optimal level of functioning. You need to take some positive action to help your system integrate the new level of frequency. A list of actions will help you identify what you need to do for your system to regain its balance.

### INTEGRATION

Each body-mind system needs some time to adjust to the new and higher energy level. Many people feel threatened by the life force and cancel out any increase in vitality through the culture's established discharge mechanisms, such as excessive eating, alcohol, cigarettes, obsessive shopping, or a retreat to television or computers.

After a session, some clients feel immediately uplifted and enjoy a direct increase in vigor and vitality. Others need more time to clear old programs. Physical, mental or emotional cleansing can manifest as a fever, cold, cough, sore throat, headache, nausea or diarrhea. It is usually an intense reaction that only lasts a short time. Some clients feel vulnerable, anxious, oversensitive and inclined to cry, or have vivid dreams or nightmares.

With experience you gain confidence that your frequency system is guiding the self-healing process and will adjust and integrate whatever comes up in a session.

## MUSCLE CHECKING BIOFEEDBACK SYSTEM

In Holographic Repatterning, the muscle checking biofeedback system is the procedure used to access information. You may know of it from working with a kinesiologist or chiropractor. To access your data bank, you use the strength or weakness shown by the muscular system, or by a specific muscle, in response to a verbal or non-verbal stimulus. This may sound incredible, but you can demonstrate it for yourself. Gently press down on a friend's outstretched arm while you are appreciating him and you will see that his arm stays strong. Use the same gentle push when you are putting him down, and his arm will become weak and collapse.

What does this mean?

In the Holographic Repatterning system, the significance of a "strong" or "weak" muscular response is that it reflects a wave pattern frequency. As I said before, the physical senses take in information from the environment in the form of frequencies. The brain evaluates the messages as positive or negative and transmits them to each cell, organ and muscle. Your whole body is a biofeedback system that constantly reacts and responds to physical, emotional and mental stimuli. You can use each muscle to find out whether either an external event or your internal response has strengthened or weakened your physical, emotional or mental system.

But not only that. We are all linked together. For this reason, you can empathetically sense what is happening in another person. You can also use your own body as a biofeedback system to access another person's 'data'. Of course, you need their permission and you should be free of personal motives and interests as to the result. If you are not neutral, you may be tempted to manipulate what comes up in a session.

The vibratory field of which we all are part is beyond space and time. Phones, radio and television use this fact to connect us across the continents. But even without modern technical support, people have been able to pick up information from other times and other places. We call it telepathy. You use it when you suddenly think of somebody and moments later you receive a letter from that person. Or when you feel that a disaster is coming your way.

In the six step process, the practitioner uses the capacity of his or her body-mind system to find out which area holds the key to your problems and self-healing. From a large data-base, they pull out information on what created and sustains the problem and determines your thinking, feeling and acting. The database contains information on unconscious responses to earlier experiences, including beliefs and survival strategies, your history over many generations, archetypal patterns and unresolved energy constrictions within the chakra and meridian systems. The practitioner examines which positive intention will help you solve the problem, and determines the self-healing modality which will shift your wave pattern so that you regain your optimal frequency level of functioning in regard to the issue at hand.

The quality of information disclosed does not depend on your both being in the same room. A practitioner can proxy muscle check on behalf of a person who is miles away by using his or her own body system to access the necessary information. It is as easy as turning on a radio or television and listening to broadcasts from thousands of miles away. In numerous sessions, Holographic Repatterning has proven that this information is consistently correct and precise. Its disclosure effectively improves the life of the person being proxied.

The muscle checking feedback system allows the practitioner to adjust the procedure to your precise situation. In each session he or she tests the different aspects of an issue and the sequence in which each aspect needs to be resolved. The procedure takes equally into account your needs and the complexity of the unconscious patterns, as well as the range of the frequency wave patterns which create our reality.

As we are all linked together, we actually share many of the issues which make life difficult and contentious. In the section about 'The Guilty Universe', I pointed out the cultural programming which results from traditional Christian beliefs and which has penetrated our body-mind system with deep-rooted feelings of guilt and shame. In the section about 'Challenges', I pointed out the disintegration of the traditional family structure which has left many people feeling lonely and isolated and deprived of a deeper meaning in their lives and which is the consequence of our socio-economic system.

A practitioner who has experience with proxy-sessions and knows how to work on a field of common issues can shift those structures for a whole group of people. Such courses are offered as a 'Group Repatterning' and 'Cultural Repatterning', where you can register for a course with a specific theme such as 'Growing through Joy', 'Relationships', 'Love and Sexuality' and others. A course runs over several months. The practitioner checks out the needs of the participants and focuses one session per week on one specific sub-theme for the whole group. You receive a summary of each session and, if you so wish, a protocol and suggestions for homework which will help you to integrate the material into your daily life.

The group and cultural repatterning helps to cause a shift in those aspects of your life that have been passed on to you by your family, the mass media or the generation chain. You may find that long standing problems are just melting away, that you are gaining new insights into the structures of some old and familiar patterns, and/or that it is becoming easier to let go of old traps and move towards new goals.[36]

# From Vision To Manifestation: The Realization Of Your Life's Purpose

### THE POWER OF THE LADY ELEPHANT

We change when we know what we want. Many people know what they do not want. By focusing on the 'do nots', they empower the undesirable. There are many reasons why people behave in this way. I have pointed out some of them in the section on 'Pitfalls'.

People with a clearly formulated objective are more successful than people who have never written down their goals. Various studies of university graduates show that over 90% of those who had stated their objectives at the end of their studies had reached them after twenty years. Out of the big group who did not write down their expectations, only a few reached their goals.

---

[36] See references at the end of the book

Why is that so?

Writing down your objective is like a commitment to yourself to reach your goals. In order to state your goals, you need to be clear, precise and aware. A goal focuses your energy and directs it. A goal allows you to overcome difficult situations.

A goal is like the lady elephant in the story of the elephant whose leg had been tied to a stake all his life. One day the rope was taken off, but the elephant did not move. All attempts to get him going failed. All explanations about his new freedom proved to be ineffective. Until one day, walking by on the far horizon, he saw the most beautiful lady elephant that he could imagine. He forgot his tied leg and ran off.

In one way or another, most people cultivate a tied leg. The tied leg can be the children or the partner, relatives or friends in need of care, or physical weaknesses and disease. We do not usually run short of excuses for our inability to move on, no matter how miserable our situation. We lack the lady elephant to inspire us and get us going.

Many people linger in 'Luck's Waiting-room', as Hildegard Knef calls it in one of her songs. "They are waiting here since yesterday for the luck that comes tomorrow, and they dream the dreams of the day after tomorrow, forgetting that it is still today. Oh! The poor, poor people".[37]

Waiting for the lady elephant does not bring her to you. You need to take the necessary steps to discover what you would like to manifest in your life.

In the section on 'Self-Realization', I pointed to the different stages of development which help us pin down the next areas that will challenge our growth. In this section I suggest goals and steps to manifest your life's purpose.

## RECOGNIZE YOUR LIFE'S PURPOSE

If I look at my life, there is a word that runs like a red thread through many of my experiences. It is the word 'Love'. Love in my life is like the turtle in the Mandelbrot-set. In every experience, be it small or big, love shines forth as a leading theme. I know all the steps, in all their beautiful and painful sides, from needy love to the universal principle.

---

[37] In German, the song is in rhyme.

In my seminars I discovered that many people could write a similar motto for their life. For some it is love, for others trust, justice, hope, fairness, openness, wisdom, luck, wealth, fulfillment, integrity, truth, creativity, beauty, humanness, harmony, health or freedom. You could continue the list. You understand the sort of qualities I am talking about.

Think about the motto for your life, or its present phase. Can you name it without having to think much about it? If not, I suggest a little exercise which will help you approach your guiding principle.[38]

## Exercise

➤ Without thinking too much, put down on a piece of paper all the qualities which you like about yourself. Name at least ten. Then underline between three and five of the central attributes. From this group, you circle the word which is the most important to you at the moment. This is the first step.

Make a second list showing all the activities through which you express yourself in the world. Ask yourself:

▷ *What do I like doing or what would I like to do, or do more of?*

➤ Select from this group the three activities that are most important to you. This is the second step.

Now close your eyes and let the world you live in emerge before your inner eye. Ask yourself:

▷ *How would the world look if I could shape it just as I wished?*

➤ Again, choose the three most important qualities. This is the third step.

---

[38] I owe ideas and techniques of this chapter to my colleagues in Findhorn with whom I developed the course: *Realizing and Living Your Life Purpose*

▶ Now bring the qualities you have underlined and circled together into one sentence. Begin with the words:

My life's purpose is to express and apply my

_____(the words of the first step)

I do this by

_____(the activities of the second step)

to create a world that

_____(the qualities of the third step)


## ENGAGE YOUR INNER GUIDE

If you felt inspired by the section about choices, you should consider what choice you need to make at this point in your life. Be honest. It won't help you to over- or underestimate your present position. If you want to travel from New York to Chicago and you make the false assumption that you are in Boston, you won't arrive in Chicago. You can of course correct the route when you notice that you have chosen the wrong starting point. Route corrections belong to life. Do not feel discouraged if you do not know exactly where you are. Just be as honest as possible.

Engage your inner guide. Ask him or her where you are in your life and listen to the answer. If you do not know how to deal with the inner guide, go back to the section called 'The Journey To The Inner Wisdom' and the one called 'Holographic Analysis'.

Take the time to go into the stillness. Words, knowledge and answers form in the stillness. If you do not succeed right away, remember that this is only a question of practice – and of letting go. Answers often emerge unexpectedly. You meet somebody who passes on a new idea; you read a page in a book that you happen to open; you pick up a sentence from a television program; you get an insight out of the blue. The diversity of options is infinite. Do not restrict them by determining the way in which you expect the answer to come.

**Exercise**

▶ Ask your inner guide, what is it that is important for you at this point in your life? If you start thinking about the whole gamut of choices, ask yourself:

▷ *What is the choice that I need to make now?*

*How am I avoiding that decision?*

*What would help me to decide?*

For example, if you are choosing to avoid action, you may be afraid of running into authority conflicts. In that case, your avoidance strategy is on the same level as your choice. You could also be afraid of hurting somebody (interpersonal area), of making a mistake (personal area) or of losing your financial base (physical area). Determine the level to which your avoidance strategy belongs, because there lies the solution. Write down everything that comes to mind which would support a positive choice. Select the most important aspect and use the techniques described in the following sections on Visualization and Next Steps to work out the solution.

## VISUALIZE YOUR GOAL

If you could decide your destiny, what would your ideal life look like? Which reality would you like to create? Remember the section about the conscious universe? Your thoughts create your world.

We know from psychological research that our body-mind responds to thoughts and feelings about an event just as if the event had actually happened. If you are afraid of an exam, your brain cannot distinguish between your mind's fear of failure and the actual failure. It will respond in the same way. You can use this brain characteristic, which you apply unconsciously, to produce the positive results in your life that you wish for. All you need to do is to understand the same principle and consciously apply it.

Visualization is the most effective way of bringing what you want into manifestation. Visualization is the process of making mental images. These mental images serve as a blueprint out of which your future will unfold.[39]

---

[39] I owe the following instructions to Maria and Roger Benson: *Creative Partnerships*, based on Robert Fritz: *DMA. Technologies of Creating*. See also his book: *The Path of Least Resistance: Learning to Become the Creative Force in Your Own Life*. Fawcett Books 1989

As a first step, you create an ideal image of how you wish your future life to be. Make it clear. This is not day dreaming, but the conscious and precise work of conceptualisation. You fill your ideal objective with more and more details so that the image becomes more and more complete and vivid. See it with your inner eye just as you would see a picture on your living-room wall. Embrace it with your senses. Taste it, touch it, smell it, listen to its sounds, so that it becomes as real as your present existence. The more you can bring your senses into play and the more you can create it as a tangible reality, the better are your chances of manifesting it in your everyday life. Then you attach to it your desire and willingness to persevere. In this way you draw forth all the resources necessary to bring your ideal into material form. Within this process of conceptualization, visualization and manifestation, you refine and concretize the image while you proceed to gather the necessary means and tools to bring the image into form.

**Exercise**

If you find it difficult to create a mental image, practice by taking simple, concrete objects first. Imagine your chair, your table or your cup of tea. Or take the photograph of a beloved person. Look at the face. Take in all the little details. And then let this face emerge in front of your inner eye, focusing on all the aspects as concretely as possible. When you have gained enough skill to create clear and precise images within, you will be ready to give shape to your future.

Start with an area in your life, your work, partner, children, friends or an aspect of yourself, that you would like to change.

Start with your current situation. Use the instruction sheet (page 176) and in the left-hand column write down all the pertinent facts, but not analyses or judgments. Include both positive and negative conditions, your feelings, thoughts, preferences and dislikes. Be as honest as possible.

Look at the situation. A good question to ask is, "Who or what is the decisive factor in this situation? Other people? The circumstances? My feelings? My negative thoughts? My tied leg?"

Turn to the right-hand column. How would the situation look if you knew that you could not fail? Do not limit your imagination. And look at the details. You must write in the present tense, describing who you are, what you do and what you have in the situation. Do not write, 'I would like to be'; instead put down, 'I am'. Do not write, 'I would like to do'; put down, 'I do'. Do not write, 'I would like to have'; put down, 'I have'.

If the flow of your imagination is interrupted by such thoughts as, "This is impossible", or "This is crazy", return to the left-hand column. Such sentences are part of your present reality. Write them down and continue.

Put down everything that you would really like to be, do or have. Check your statements from time to time and ask yourself, "If I could have this, would I take it?" If your answer is 'no', change the image until you can say a wholehearted 'yes' to it.

Your vision or goal should be the clear image of a desired result.

△   Clear means that you will recognize it when it happens. A statement such as, "I would like to be happy" is too vague. Happiness means something different for each person. If happiness is one of your goals, describe what it would look like in your life;

△   Image means that you use your right brain for this process and let the result appear in front of your inner eye as a 'Gestalt';

△   Desired means that you would accept the result if you could have it;

△   Result means that you focus on a final motive and not on a process.

For example, if you desire money, you should ask yourself what you would like to do with it. Is it security or recognition that you hope money will give you? If so, then security or recognition would be the result. You may get that

# VISION
## AND
## CURRENT REALITY

My Life's purpose is to express and apply my:

_____

_____

_____

**1** Think of an area in your life that you would like to be different
(it can be a relationship, work, something in yourself etc.)

**2** Describe your current reality
(what the situation is like now)

**3** Create your vision
(a clear picture of a desired result)

**4** Summarize the description of your ideal situation in a few key words and form a
picture in your mind that represents it.

_____

_____

_____

**5** Ask yourself: If I could have (or be) this, would I take it?
If you say no, change it so that you can fully say yes to it.

**6** Notice the discrepancy between what the situation is now and your vision.
Acknowledge the 'now' and focus on your vision. This tension will always seek resolution, and in holding the focus upon your vision, the resolution will be towards
its creation.

even without the money. Allow yourself to inquire more deeply into your motives. You may say, 'I do not know what I really want'. You do not need to know. As you go all out for what is available for you now, you draw in feedback from the universe that will help you to refine and specify your goals and vision. All you need to do is to be aware of what is important for you right now. Often we can only see the next step on our path, and as we take that step, the next one unfolds.

For me, it is like painting a picture. I start with an idea of how the final result should look. In the process of painting this idea, I get immersed in the details. I step back, look at the bigger picture, and concentrate on painting the next aspect. At the end, the picture emerges in its mature form. I recognize the original idea contained in it, and at the same time it is completely different. In dialogue with the material world, paintbrush and colors have formed and specified the original concept.

Do not get fixated on your original idea or concept. The world is a dynamic interplay of unfolded and enfolded realities. Your thoughts impact those worlds, and those worlds reflect back to you. We call this dynamic a feedback system, a course correction or a learning through doing.

> ▶ If you have formed a clear picture of the desired result, summarize it in a few key words and make a picture in your mind to represent it. This process is called visualization. It engages your left and right-hand brain, your conscious and unconscious self, and unites their combined forces behind a common goal.
>
> Ask yourself at this point, "If I could have (be or do) this, would I take it?" If you say 'no', change the picture until you can say a decisive 'yes' to it.
>
> Finally... notice the discrepancy between your current reality and your vision. Acknowledge the now and focus on your vision. This creates a structural tension that will seek resolution. If you keep your mind focused on the vision, the resolution will be directed towards its creation on the material plane.

The challenge at this point is to hold the structural tension without transforming it into psychological or physical tension. Many people tend to resolve the discomfort of an inner discord by compromising the vision, or by not admitting to themselves the truth of their current reality.

If you find it difficult to hold the structural tension, begin with small steps. As you practice embracing structural tension without feeling the need to resolve it, you build up your capacity to embrace more and more.

## DETERMINE YOUR NEXT STEPS

Some people have no trouble designing beautiful visions and plans, but when it comes down to bringing them into reality, they never get manifested. You may recognize this phenomenon from all the great New Year resolutions that are never carried out. Sometimes, people lack the will-power, persistence or even the desire to manifest their intentions. And sometimes they just lack the information or experience which would tell them how to realize a vision or positive intent.

**Exercise**

▶ Begin with small steps. Ask yourself:

▷ *What step am I willing to take to realize my intention?*
*What second step am I willing to take?*

Be specific. Statements like, "I want to change my life," do not contain any valuable information. How would you know that you have changed your life if you do not specify what the change involves? General statements often serve the function of avoiding a commitment to action.

Take an honest look at what you are really willing and able to do. If you intend to change your home or working place, this can mean that you will gather information or contact particular people. If you want to improve your health, this can mean that you will do daily exercises, change your nutrition style or consult a doctor or practitioner. If you would like to clarify an unresolved issue in a relationship, this can mean that you will write a letter or make an appointment.

➤ Put down <u>exactly</u> when you will start taking your first step. Exactly means an exact time on an exact day, not tomorrow or next week.

Then ask yourself:

▷ *How do I sabotage myself from keeping my commitments to myself?*

*What 'usually' happens to prevent it? A deadline which I have overlooked? Other people's needs? My own resistance?*

Take a good look at how you normally block yourself from getting what you want in life. The better you know your 'enemy', the better your chances of overcoming your pattern of resistance.

➤ Think of situations in which you successfully outwitted your saboteur. How did you do that? Ask yourself:

▷ *What is the difference between the situations in which I keep my commitments and those in which I give my power to the saboteur?*

*How did I feel afterwards in either situation?*

*What do I decide to do this time?*

You know meanwhile that it is your choice.

Take a look at your friends and acquaintances. Who would be willing to support you in your positive intentions? Who would be willing to further these new aspects of your being? This is the point where good friends differ from normal acquaintances. If you cannot think of anybody, then this is certainly an issue into which it is worthwhile putting some thought and work.

➤ Choose your support person and arrange for a fixed time when they are there for you. With them you celebrate your successes and keep your shortcomings in check and balance.

Finally, write down the exact words of your positive intention and commitment. For this purpose, I use the following sequence:

► My intent is

_____

_____

_____

(put down the sentence that you wrote against item 4 of the instruction sheet)

and I do this by _____

_____

_____

(write down your steps)

Repeat this statement as often as you can so that your subconscious can adjust to the new result and will support you in reaching it. Place the sentence in big letters over your bed, in the kitchen and over your table or desk. Lean back, relax and give thanks for the many ways in which the universal mind helps you to realize your intent, just so long as you want to do something good with it and serve other people as much as yourself.

Relaxation, visualization and the repeated affirmation of your goal, together with thanks that the desired result is already given to you, is the secret of success and the secret recipe of growing through joy. Use it!

It is up to you, and only you, what you decide. Your body-mind acts on all your intentions, be they positive or negative. It does not have the capacity to discriminate between the two. The holograms of your brain contain your desires as well as your fears, and your aspirations as well as your doubts. Today's spiritual and technological conditions make it possible to choose between them. You can set your talents free and create the reality that you want. Do it!

# NEXT
# STEPS

This sheet is to help you to find practical steps to let your vision come true. How can you apply your insight? What are you willing to do? What else are you willing to do? Write down each step.

What's a first step you are willing to take to apply your insight to your current situation? Be specific.

_____

_____

What's another step you are willing to take?

_____

_____

When exactly will you begin?

_____

What might get in the way of you taking these steps?

_____

_____

What can you do to overcome these blocks?

_____

_____

Who will you share your next steps with? Think of a friend who can support you in following through on your commitment to let your vision, your life's purpose, come true and to nourish new aspects of your being.

My support person is _____

Write a concise statement of your main commitment in relation to your life's purpose and/or vision.

_____

_____

_____

_____

_____

_____

We live in an awesome time, a time that provides us with the understanding and tools to shift the old paradigm of suffering into a paradigm of joy. Joy is the warmth that helps melt the isolation which so many people experience and which makes them feel and behave like ice-cubes.

Joy is the quality of the heart. Many people have closed it off from fear of standing in the 'wound' of love, that wound which unites us as human beings. There is hardly anybody who has not suffered from love in at least one of its many forms, be it on a personal or collective level. The wound may be so deep and the pain so unbearable that you may wish to hide it from yourself.

To heal this wound, we need to let go of all the games and masks that we use to protect ourselves. We have to become naked so that the soul can break through the shell of isolation and unite again with the flow of life. That is where the tears of pain and the tears of joy blend with each other and become one.

If we open up to the flow of life, if we allow the pulsation of life to nourish our body and to guide the cycle of our life, we move beyond the judgments, guilt and shame that lie at the root of suffering.

If we flow with life, it will bring us all we need. Our vision will open up to embrace the purpose of our soul and of our life. The opening of the heart with its qualities of love and joy will attract all that is needed to fulfill this purpose. Our mind will start to grasp the cyclic nature of life and deepen its understanding as we follow the journey of the soul back to its source.

Within this process we are supported by the spirit and evolution of this time. According to many prophecies ranging from the Bible to the Maya, we are about to begin the journey backwards to our source, which will take the next 1.2 billion years of earth time. Within our present time, many forces that are not visible to our eyes are helping us to move beyond the established and deep-rooted cultural patterns which have governed our lives for the last millennia. As more and more people move through those shifts, they create a field of consciousness that allows yet more to move with them in an exponential torrent.

Thanks to the invisible support system and the rapidly growing collective consciousness, we have the opportunity to overcome the old conditionings and ways of learning through suffering and pain, and to open up to love and joy as the main tools for growth. This will not happen just by itself. We still have to take steps which express our commitment to making the shift happen. We will then pull in those forces that will speed up our learning curve and open up possibilities undreamed of.

May the tools and the understanding offered in this book help you to draw to you everything that will make your life fulfilled.

# References for Holographic Repatterning

**For more information about Cultural repatterning and for bookings, visit my website:**

www.visioform.com

**For information on Seminars, Group Repatterning and Certified Practitioners in Holographic Repatterning in USA, visit:**

www.repatterning.com

**or write to:**    HR Association,
P.O. Box 204,
Glorieta, NM 87535
USA
e-mail: hra@holographic.org
fax: 505 757 3140
phone: 505 757 3883

**For information on Group Repatterning in UK, write to:**

Lori Forsyth
Healthworks, 5 Bank Lane,
Forres, IV36 1NU.
e-mail: loribruce@findhorn.org

**For information on Seminars and Certified Practitioners in UK write to:**

HR Association, UK
c/o Anne Kille, People Development
e-mail: annk@enterprise.net
Mobile phone: 0973 890052

# Further Reading

Becker, Anthea: *Holographic Repatterning Handbook*. Sedona 1994

Braden, Gregg: *Awakening to Zero Point. The Collective Initiation*. Sacred Spaces/Ancient Wisdom. Mexico 1994

Chia, Mantak & Maneewan: *Taoist Ways to Transform Stress into Vitality*. Huntington: Healing Tao Books 1985

Crystal, Phyllis: *Cutting the Ties that Bind: Growing Up and Moving On*. York Beach: Samuel Weiser 1994

Fritz, Robert: *The Path of Least Resistance: Learning to Become the Creative Force in Your Own Life*. New York: Fawcett Books 1989

Fieger, Leslie: *The Delfin System*. Alexandra. Delfin International 1995

Goel, Bhim S. *Psychoanalysis and Meditation*. New Delhi: Paragon Enterprises 1986

Jacobi, Jolan: *The Psychology of C.G.Jung*. London: Kegan Paul et al. 1942

Rinpoche, Sogyal: *The Tibetan Book of Living and Dying*. London: Rider 1992

Sebastian, Ulla: *Erfahrungen mit Sai Baba in Indien (Experiences with Sai Baba in India* (German text)). München: Goldmann 1992

Sills, Franklyn: *The Polarity Process*. Shaftesbury: Element Books 1989

Snow. Chet B. and Helen Wambach: *Mass Dreams of the Future*. New York: McGraw-Hill 1989

Stone, Joshua D.: *The Complete Ascension Manual*. Sedona: Light Technology Publishing 1994

Talbot, Michael: *The Holographic Universe*. New York: HarperCollins 1991

Wilber, Ken: *Sex, Ecology, Spirituality*. Boston & London: Shambala 1995

Woolf, V. Vernon: *Holodynamics*. Tuscon: Harbinger 1990

Wordsworth, Chloe: *Holographic Repatterning. Model and Process for Positive Change and Transformation*. Sedona 1994

# Index